the good your money can do

Becoming a Conscious Investor

Eva Yazhari

THE

conscious

INVESTOR

——— PRESS ———

THE GOOD YOUR MONEY CAN DO
Becoming a Conscious Investor

ISBN   978-1-5445-0991-4 *Hardcover*
   978-1-5445-0990-7 *Paperback*
   978-1-5445-0989-1 *Ebook*
   978-1-5445-0992-1 *Audiobook*

disclaimer

This book does not constitute investment advice. My goal is to provide the tools for you, the reader, to find interest, inspiration, and education in the topic of impact investing. Therefore, *The Good Your Money Can Do* is for inspirational and informational purposes only. It is in no way intended to substitute for professional investment advice, professional financial advice, or general counsel. To the extent that any section of this book features the insight, opinions, or advice of an expert or company, the expressed views are those of the cited person or company and do not necessarily represent my opinion or that of my affiliates. Further, the examples in this book are largely oriented around the U.S. market and do not serve as examples for other markets where options may differ.

I dedicate this book to the people who have been marginalized by systems that do not work equitably for all the members of our global human family. The practice of conscious investing has made me feel more connected to you and illuminated that we are united in the impact we can have.

contents

foreword

Why become a "conscious investor," anyway?

Here's why: because money is a form of currency, and currency is energy.[1]

Literally, your money and other resources carry an energetic charge. This charge can be positive, leading to meaning and a stable society, or it can be negative, leading to unhappy individuals. To be conscious is to become emotionally aware of the charge within your resources in relation to the energy you intend to have in the world. Basically, just watch what you spend it on—as it will reveal what you care about.

That's why being conscious about money, currency, and, indeed, *all* financial investments matters. To be unconscious about your money and investments is to neglect to recognize the fact that *money is a form of currency and currency is energy* and, therefore, to wield the power of your resources without intention or purpose. To be conscious is to create more of what you really want: meaning, harmony, and even happiness.

This book shows you how to do just that, suggesting that to examine your investments, at least from time to time, will help you to make corrections to your course and to align them with your values. Occasionally, examining your money's path may even call you to really look at your life's path, as Eva once did herself. As she details in this book, though she had grown up with the examples of service and altruism in her own family, her trajectory first included a stint as a capitalist, where although she learned many valuable skills, she didn't always feel that her work was in alignment with her values. It was only years later, emboldened by what she was seeing in the management of her own money, that she decided to gracefully challenge the narrow focus of investment for the sake of nothing more than returns. That's when she discovered her own calling: expanding her family's portfolio to—among other areas—support the environment and empower business creation in impoverished nations, with great success. And now, she is generously bestowing this upon you.

If you are ready to become conscious, it is wise, perhaps, to begin by identifying money, financial investments, and other resources that can be exchanged for products, services, and, indeed, goods, as something that does carry an emotional charge. To this end, all you need to do is consider that money only exists as a means for exchange because society has agreed to this concept, an "intersubjective reality," that is unalterably social.[2] That means money and other resources can impact society, both positively and negatively. The way you spend and invest has such power.

If you will follow this thread, you may agree next to consider that a lack of consciousness in capitalism—the kind that only survives for gains at anything's and anyone's expense—has effects, some negative. You can't say Adam Smith didn't warn us of this possibility: as with many other Enlightenment thinkers, Smith believed in the idea that a stable society is required for there to be any hope of human progress. In *The Wealth of Nations*, he made the case that anything that threatens the breakdown of that primary stability is not a risk worth taking. In this sense, the pursuit of returns and no other value as a motivator devoid of consciousness is not a self-interest that works because it threatens our stability as a society.

We also know that financial returns have no lasting effect on happiness either.[3] Take it from a personal and executive coach: I've seen up close that money not only doesn't buy happiness, but that the nuances of its use are extremely telling toward your outcomes. Becoming more conscious about what your money does and where it goes is a win-win.

Here's the point: money is a fantastic tool. I like it, and I hope you do too. It can bless people with all kinds of possibilities and freedom. But all it is is a means to an end, not *the* end. The love of life and of each other is the end. Thinking about money in this way and becoming aware of your beliefs and values around this most ubiquitous of tools is a life-changing activity. Do yourself a favor and join this book's powerful discussion, using the many ideas contained within as your path to the creation of meaning. This will have practical and surprising consequences for your life.

You'll see.

—Keren Eldad

Keren Eldad is a Transformational Leadership Coach and Founder of With Enthusiasm® Coaching, as well as a Professional Speaker and Host of the Coached Podcast.

introduction

"Why would you want to take this investment out of your portfolio?"

My investment advisor was all smiles. We were sitting across from each other in a beautiful conference room overlooking Lake Zurich in the sophisticated Swiss banking city. It was the fall of 2011. For months, I had been telling him that I wanted my investments to align more with my values, explaining that much of the rest of my life was already in alignment. But he was not getting the message.

I tried again. "I do not want to own part of a large tobacco company. It is not what I consider a life-affirming investment. There are plenty of other opportunities to make money."

He politely waved me off, laying his best investor-speak on my husband and me.

"But this is a good debt investment for you, and it fits into your portfolio return mandate," he said.

I wanted to object again, but I could already tell he would not listen. Soon, the meeting was over, and we had politely talked about my life savings as if they belonged to a person with different values than my own. Walking out of the office, I felt as if I had been shamed for demanding more from my money, for wanting to live by *my* values, and for questioning the judgment of an experienced wealth advisor.

Worse than that, I felt powerless. I cared deeply about where my money was invested. In fact, I had staked my whole career on the idea that it could be invested in alignment with my principles. Five years earlier, I had left my career on Wall Street, moved to Zurich with my husband for his career, and pivoted to pursue impact investing, a growing approach to investing based on using your resources to create a positive impact. In the years that followed, I had fully committed to aligning all areas of my life with my values and living more sustainably. I knew that I still had a ways to go to get where I wanted to be, but I also knew that I had done a lot of good with my money in a relatively short amount of time—and the pursuit was possible.

All of that felt insignificant now. If I could not get my investment advisor to listen to me, then what good was I doing? Despite my best intentions, was I nothing more than a hypocrite?

That night, something struck me: my financial advisor thought he was doing what was right. He was trying his best to be a fiduciary of my capital and guide me toward my financial goals. I had explained my vision for my investment portfolio to him, but he did not understand what I meant by "impact investing" or how to apply it to my portfolio. To him, the purpose of investment management was to make more money or, at least, to preserve capital. Impact investing was nothing more than a soft discipline as far as he was concerned.

That got me thinking: I was frustrated that this smart, well-known advisor at a reputable Swiss bank did not understand what I was driving toward. However, I also knew that he was not the exception but rather the norm. Despite the fact that impact investing comprises more than a quarter of all investing, most people still did not know what it was or how to practice it, and many groups that focus on educating investors target large wealth holders, which most of us are not.

My mind flashed back to a presentation I had given several months before at a conference in Brussels. I was speaking to an audience of about fifty, all of whom were highly successful French and Belgian businesspeople. Confidently, I had launched into my presentation, but within moments, an audience member raised his hand.

"Excuse me, but what exactly is impact investing?"

Others chimed in. Within moments, it was clear that not a single person in the room had any idea what I was talking about. So, for the rest of the presentation, I walked them through it. It was not the talk I had planned, but for them, it was a revelation. Afterward, it was like a switch had been flipped in their heads. These professionals had never heard of impact investing until that day. But now that they had, they were all fascinated by the concept and the ability to think differently about their money.

The more I got to thinking, the more I realized that impact investing, while a growing and increasingly valued practice, had an awareness deficit. Most people I know would love to leverage their money toward a cause that is important to them, but outside of philanthropy, they are not aware that such opportunities exist.

Perhaps this describes you as well. Like my audience in Brussels, you are interested in using your money to make a difference, but you are not sure how. Or, like my investment advisor, you have heard of impact investing, but until now, you have not taken it seriously. Or, you are neither, and you just picked up this book because you like the idea of using your money to do good.

Whatever the case, I wrote this book to show you the value impact investing can create in your life—and the tremendous difference it can have for others and the planet.

you can do good with your money

Most of us are taught that there are only three ways we can use our money: save it, invest it, or spend it. Each is important in its own right, but there is another way you can utilize your resources. You can use it to make change—good or bad.

Impact investing is a means for creating a positive impact. Specifically, impact investing is the process of investing with the intent of creating positive change—be it social, technological, or environmental—all while earning a financial return. It is a way to look beyond your money to help find meaning and purpose in your life and the issues you care about. It is a way to be proud of how you invest your money—and to inspire others to do the same.

Equally important to what impact investing can do for others is what impact investing can do for you. It feels wonderful to do good.

Impact investing gives focus to our inherent desire to make the world a better place. And in so doing, it creates an upward spiral of pride and accomplishment in our lives.

From a young age, I was fortunate to witness the sense of pride and empowerment that came from doing good. My childhood was filled with stories of how my grandfather moved his family of six (including an infant!) from Michigan to the remote town of Kisa, Tanzania, so he could start a health clinic. Some stories, like the one about my father's pet monkey, were charming and whimsical. Others have impacted me in ways I may never fully appreciate, like the day my grandfather adopted a little girl into the family after her mother died in childbirth. My aunt remains a vital part of our family, and I could not imagine not knowing her and her children.

My family's time in Tanzania ended before I was born, but their legacy of service has lived on. By the time I was born, my parents lived as artists in New York City. Growing up in that rich creative environment—full of afternoons in my father's studio and week-end visits to prominent galleries—I learned the value not only of art but also of the artists who create it. The rich creativity of my upbringing lent itself to my current type of investing that values creativity in the investment process. I have seen firsthand how it is possible to invest both in business and in people—specifically in their creativity and desire to create greater impact and live more satisfying lives.

With this background, it is, perhaps, no surprise that when I entered adulthood and began my career in financial analysis, I felt like something was missing. I was good at my job and all the due diligence and rigor that came with it, but I could not help feeling that my finance skills could be better applied to something more than just making money. In my finance career, I was observing investors of all kinds utilizing their money to make change, and I thought it had to be possible to affect change on other levels. I wanted to contribute beyond myself, and if finance was a tool, why could it not be applied to positive impact?

As this idea persisted in my head, I began to look to my relationships for guidance. When my husband, Hooman, and I first met, we quickly realized that we shared the same vision of equality and creating a greater social and environmental impact together. However, we always saw this vision as something we would pursue in the future, rather than in the moment. One night over dinner, we looked at each other and asked, "Why are we waiting?" If we could pursue this effort now rather than later, then we *should*. So, in early 2009, I left Wall Street to pursue impact investing as a career. By May, we had founded Beyond Capital, an impact investment venture capital fund focused on improving the lives of those living under the global poverty line.

Inspired by my family's time in Tanzania, I saw Beyond Capital as an opportunity to apply new approaches to alleviating poverty while maximizing my own personal impact. If I could find a way to use my skills to help those living below the global poverty line, then I could contribute to positive social, environmental, technological, and governance outcomes in a way that was consistent with my own skills and values.

becoming a conscious investor

With sixteen years of investment, entrepreneurship, and leadership experience that goes beyond conventions, I feel a strong desire to connect my money with my own values. I launched Beyond Capital in 2009 to do just that, and in the years since, we have grown to become a recognized global brand with a successful track record.

Further, in the context of our increasingly global world, I noticed that my networks were asking more questions and searching for purpose. However, something was missing. Both the investors and friends I spoke to all lacked a connection to meaning in their money and resources. It was clear that a knowledge gap existed not only between impact investment insiders and outsiders but also among these insiders themselves. This is unfortunate, given the tools of capitalism available and the fact that impact investing can be accessible to anyone. Every day, I encounter people who wish that their money—be it their retirement savings, investment accounts, or savings—were more aligned with their values. We are all looking for ways to leverage our money to help bring meaning and purpose to our lives, yet many of us are not sure how.

The more I became aware of this knowledge gap, the more passionate I became about changing it. Since co-founding Beyond Capital, I have set out to do this in two key ways: The first was to address the many pressing challenges within finance and to make impact investing more accessible. In my work, I have found that a ground-up approach to addressing this need does not fully exist. Either there are barriers to enter the market as an impact inve or the solution to helping others find purpose in their money is too institutional, which may not resonate with them. Mainstream advisors and banks are used to telling clients how they should invest, rather than asking how they *want* to invest. Instead of partnering with clients to compose solutions together, they present them with prepackaged options that often do not fit their needs, their passions, or their desires.

The second was to begin speaking to a wider audience about impact investing. Over the last few years, I have been moved to share the stories of dozens of high-performing CEOs on *The Beyond Capital Podcast* and in-depth analyses of different facets of conscious living through *The Conscious Investor* magazine. *The Beyond Capital Podcast*, which I cohost with serial entrepreneur and Preciate CEO Ed Stevens, features candid conversations with purpose-driven leaders that explore how and why profit can be married with purpose, while *The Conscious Investor* is a weekly magazine featuring wisdom and inspiration to help readers find purpose in their money. This experience working on this podcast and magazine, along with the many conversations I have had with those I have met along the way, have served as inspiration for writing this book.

This impetus became all the more urgent as I first began writing in early 2020. right as the COVID-19 pandemic began spreading ac̱ ̱. During this intense time, humanity's priorities ̱ocus of many became more global. 2020 was a ̱ faced protests, wide-scale fires, and a pivotal ̱d States. The moral imperative was heightened. ̱nd awareness expanded, our basic needs were underscored, and society was put to the test. I saw the COVID-19 pandemic as a harbinger for forthcoming challenges that we could face. As my friend, Paul Van Zyl, points out, "Climate change is coronavirus without a vaccine." With so much needed to build back better and move beyond the pandemic, I believe the time is right to share how we can all be a part of that movement.

This book, then, is my contribution to that movement, an opportunity to activate greater impact by educating you to the possibilities of impact investing—and how, by learning to navigate this practice, you can become what I refer to as a *conscious investor*. I want to open up the conversation about what you can do with your money and demonstrate how becoming a conscious investor can be used to create the change you want to see. By taking a more proactive approach to the consciousness of your capital, you can bring conversations about impact investing from the fringe to the mainstream.

To that end, I have divided this book into two parts. Part 1, "The Power of Conscious Investing," is a framework for thinking about the concepts and ideas that shape the work. Here, I will make the case for impact investing—how it works, why investors have a moral imperative to embrace this approach, and how it can be leveraged to not only create good but also help you find meaning and purpose in your life. Money may be one of the primary vehicles of impact investing, but money is also just a means to an end. At its core, conscious investing is a framework for those looking to find more meaning and purpose in their life and to help them recognize the good they can do with their money.

This framework is essential if you want to be effective as a conscious investor. After all, the world is in need of a lot of change. Without clarity on how impact investing operates and how you can be most effective within it, you may find that you are spending a great deal of energy but creating very little impact. Part 1 provides an opportunity to look within yourself and be inspired by other successful conscious investors and purpose-driven business owners, who have refined their own strategies, learned to pinpoint what they want to focus on, and in so doing, have learned how to create measurable impact in those areas.

Part 2, "What Can You Do Today?", is a playbook for action. Here, I will take you through a step-by-step approach to begin building the mindset and the practices necessary for becoming a conscious investor. By embracing a mindset of wealth consciousness, you will learn to be proactive about what you own, to clearly define your values, and to take real steps to live by them. I have also included an appendix at the end, which ties the people and organizations discussed in this book to the Sustainable Development Goals (SDGs) they represent and advocate for.

getting started

This book is for readers with at least some financial resources—be it a portfolio, a retirement savings, or savings—who are curious about doing more with their capital, curious about the good their money can do, and curious about how to bring their personal values to their money. This does not mean you must have over $250,000 per investment to get value from this book. However, it does mean that you are actively saving or that you are otherwise actively growing your wealth.

To be clear, money is not the only way to think about the good you can do. As you will see, the concept of wealth as used in this book does not just apply to financial wealth. However, consider this your guidebook if you have begun to realize that true wealth has to do with more than just money—it can also include consumer choices, time, relationships, networks, mindsets, and world view—and that you can more directly leverage that wealth by becoming an impact investor, or a conscious investor. Thinking more broadly about your wealth will help you feel more complete about your approach.

If you are already an impact investor with a systematic approach, this book can help you learn the simple tools and frameworks to easily share with others. If, however, you are a practicing impact investor, who is looking to refine what you are doing, or you are otherwise looking for some new ideas or a broader perspective, I encourage you to read on. Similarly, if you have been an impact investor for a while and you know somebody who you would like to introduce to conscious investing and offer a framework for getting started, this book can help you learn those tools so that you might share them with others.

As you set out on your path to becoming a conscious investor, I want you to remember a few important facts.

First, the barrier to entry is relatively low. Anyone with even a small amount of investment capital can become a conscious investor, not just the tech entrepreneurs and billionaires who often dominate financial conversations. Regardless of where you come from—regardless of your background, political views, religion, gender, or anything else—you have the opportunity to invest your time, money, and resources in ways that align with your values and contribute beyond yourself.

Second, while getting started is easy, conscious investing is not a quick-fix solution. Rather, it is a lifelong experience of self-improvement and self-discovery. Like me, you may encounter advisors who do not understand your goals and are not willing to help. Or you may find that your approach to impact investing, while well-intentioned, may not actually be creating the positive impact that you hoped it would or the financial return that you expected.

Whatever happens, I encourage you to keep moving forward. As with many worthwhile endeavors, setbacks are just part of the process. Rather than feel discouraged in these moments, instead use them as opportunities to redefine and refocus your goals. In so doing, you will bring clarity to your efforts. Just remember that any time you can define what you *do not* want, you are a step closer to better understanding what you *do* want.

It is also important to note that impact investing is not a one-size-fits-all approach. Different people will get different results, each relative to their own means, values, and ability to contribute. It is not a matter of who does the most good or who lives the most value-aligned life. It is about practicing wealth consciousness, learning about our investment choices, and feeling empowered to make decisions that reflect our values and contribute to positive change.

Above all, it is about patience. Impact investing rewards a systematic approach—and that takes time. However, with the stories and lessons in this book serving as your roadmap, you too can create a life in which your money and your values are aligned.

All that is left to do now is get started.

part 1

the power of conscious investing

I am often asked how I know impact investing is for me. What about philanthropy or other charitable endeavors? First of all, impact investing is for you if you care about making a positive impact. It is that simple. Even if your only asset is the money in your bank account, you can choose a socially conscious bank and put your money to work that way. Impact investing is just another tool for anyone: new investors, experienced investors, conscious consumers, and curious citizens. Unless your cash is sitting under a mattress, it is having an impact in some way; the key is to understand that, know that impact investing can fuel meaning and purpose in your life, and understand what is possible.

Before getting started, it is paramount to understand that you do not need to sacrifice returns if you select your investments to be in line with your return expectations. You can absolutely meet most financial return expectations—you are just asking more from your investments and asking your money to work harder for you. It is also key to learn how to integrate positive impact into your daily work life and how to avoid going back to business as usual, knowing that using your investments as a tool for good will serve you and those around you. Finally, there are so many innovations and reasons to get involved, but ultimately, the path is yours to take. After exploring the power of conscious investing in Part 1, you will be inspired and ready to get started.

WHY CONSCIOUS INVESTING MATTERS

1. Understanding what conscious investing is and how it fits into the financial ecosystem
2. Clarifying meaning and purpose in our lives and how contributing beyond ourselves fuels happiness
3. Addressing social and environmental challenges with sustainable innovations and practicing being wealth conscious
4. Setting the foundation to get started

CHAPTER 1

the case for
conscious investing

"You really inspired me up there," the woman beside me said with a smile. "I had never thought to ask about what I own."

That day, I was cohosting a gathering that was focused on inspiring the creative community to think about integrating impact investing into their work and lives. During my presentation, I spoke about the power impact investing can have, which I expected would be a new topic for most in the room. Later at lunch, the woman sitting next to me explained just how new a topic it was.

Like many investors, she had no idea what was in her investment portfolio. Occasionally, she had worried that her portfolio might not be consistent with her values. Specifically, she was concerned that some of the investments in her portfolio did not promote gender equality, a value she held very closely. Despite this concern, she never considered what she might be able to do about it. After hearing what might be possible with more intentional investments, she decided it was time to learn.

Her candor and vulnerability—how willingly she admitted her lack of understanding and how determined she had become to change that—inspired me. That morning, she had never heard of impact investing, and by lunchtime, she was willing to take the first step.

Investments are about saving for the future and growing capital over time. To be fair, if that is all you choose to think about, that is all it has to be. But it can be so much more. She knew just how much potential was ahead of her, and by the end of this book, my goal is for you to internalize this understanding as well.

It just took one question to change her entire investment paradigm, and I believe the same is true for you. Simply ask yourself: *What do I own?* Then, sit with the answer, whether or not it is clear.

Understanding what you own and how your money is being used is at the heart of impact investing.

Related to the philosophy of *wealth consciousness*, impact investing is the revolutionary idea that money has the potential to create an impressive social, environmental, or ethical impact and that you can choose to be intentional and purposeful with how you use that power. Without this awareness, money becomes a goal in itself, without regard for purpose or creating positive impact. In that scenario, as too many of us have experienced, you can never find fulfillment or have "enough."

Once you do become aware of the power your investments hold, great responsibility follows. The next step is to analyze whether those investments align with what you believe and, most importantly, what you might choose to own instead.

the limits of the existing paradigm

When most people think about having an impact with their money, they often think about philanthropy—the act of giving to charities, nonprofits, and important causes. To the public at large, this remains the standard method of positive impact.

While there are times when philanthropy is the best solution for a social problem, it comes with limitations that constrain potential impact—namely, that sums donated to philanthropic organizations will not grow over time in the way that an investment can. Further, impact investing takes a more solutions-focused approach to a problem, allowing you to invest in practices, products, services, and technologies that will one day become self-sustainable. Finally, while nonprofits receive over an estimated $400 billion in donations every year, impact investing is able to tap other potential funding sources—specifically, investment capital—that can then be directed toward doing good.[4]

Entrepreneur, activist, and fundraiser Dan Pallotta argues in a powerful TED Talk that the way we think about philanthropy actually undermines the causes we are hoping to support. He lays out five areas of discrimination against nonprofits (including team compensation and advertising and marketing spend) that make it difficult for nonprofits to scale their work. Since 1970, the for-profit sector has grown substantially while poverty has not declined.[5] As a conscious investor who has experience running a nonprofit, I can tell you that my for-profit counterparts do not receive the constant questions about operations, overhead, and admin expenses that I am faced with. These questions are often counterproductive, and they constrain the work that I (and others) in the nonprofit sector are trying to do.

In fact, it is often concerns like these that make others hesitant to venture into impact investing. As Pallotta observes, the thought of people making money helping other people often elicits a visceral reaction. Society often has unrealistic expectations when it comes to our nonprofit organizations, which are often capital constrained and not purely market driven. And yet, despite these expectations, a belief persists that morality equates to frugality. People are wary of being asked to do the least that they can possibly do—though, at the same time, they are yearning to measure the full distance of their potential on behalf of the causes they care deeply about. If we are constantly asking nonprofits to reduce their budgets and be frugal—which will inhibit the change they want to see—then there has to be another way.

Meanwhile, for all of the scrutiny, philanthropic money is often given unsystematically. As researchers and Nobel laureates Abhijit Banerjee, Esther Duflo, and Michael Kremer found, most participants in philanthropy (whether governments, non-governmental organizations, or individual donors) do not take a scientific or evidence-based approach with their efforts. Instead of focusing on the areas of greatest need, in ways that can create the most impact and in ways that actually serve the communities they profess to help, they are often just as haphazard, reactive, and unintentional as an impersonal wealth portfolio. While high net worth families give 15 percent of philanthropic money to the arts and 25 percent to education, they only give 4 percent to basic needs like food and shelter—and even less to food security and access to healthcare.[6]

Further, according to political scientist Rob Reich, philanthropy can also be seen as an exercise of plutocratic bias, a tool for those with means to funnel money into the "think tanks, advocacy groups, litigation outfits, voter mobilization organizations, and media outlets—on both the left and right—that amplify the preferences of wealth holders in public life."[7] In this view, philanthropy is not only inefficient but undemocratic, allowing citizens with means to have a disproportionate influence in what causes matter and what do not— often to the detriment of historically marginalized communities.

In recent years, microfinance has emerged as a more intentional, impactful alternative to direct donations. This practice was first made popular by Muhammad Yunus, who lent twenty-seven dollars to forty-two different women in his village in the 1970s. Each loan made him a very small profit, helping him become the first person to finance others' small businesses and launch his career as a leader in the field of scaled positive impact.

Microfinance is powerful in its ability to lend essential support to small businesses, especially to those in nations that some might consider less developed. A sum less than twenty-seven dollars might not sound like much, but to the women that Yunus lent the money to, it often made the difference between success or failure for their businesses, helping them to pay for important assets or grow their business in small ways.

Millions of Americans have also felt the power of microfinance as a tool for doing good. A great example is Kiva, one of the most ubiquitous microfinance organizations, which allows donors to re-lend money over time and support small businesses on a monthly basis. With a growing pool of businesses spanning the globe, Kiva allows investors to offer their support to women in education, to businesses in conflict zones, and to many other specific areas of need. This connects people of completely different backgrounds and cultures to unite them as one human family. To date, Kiva has helped generate over $1.5 billion in microfinance, with loans starting as low as twenty-five dollars.

Kiva has proven a powerful lending tool, allowing citizens to directly feel the power of giving in a sustainable, systematic way. In fact, Kiva has had such a positive effect on the public consciousness that it is usually the first comparison people make when I introduce the concept of impact investing. After all, most individuals love helping where they can and are usually surprised and thrilled to not only see that money come back to them, but that they can then turn around and reinvest that money in another deserving business.

As wonderful as organizations like Kiva are, there are limitations to microfinance as well, not the least of which is the *micro* component. There is only so much microfinance can accomplish, and those hoping to make a larger impact with their money may find it lacking or not comprehensive (for example, the opportunity to make impact investments in infrastructure that allow for access to energy in rural areas).

More recently, impact investing has emerged as a powerful complement, blending the cause-based, value-focused nature of philanthropy with the results-oriented approach of microfinance. Impact investing scales our ability to do good, creating an exponentially larger impact than any other form of giving can create.

what is impact investing?

Impact investing can take many forms, from buying stock in cause-based companies to investing resources other than money to create a meaningful impact. For instance, a conscious investor interested in combating climate change might invest in green real estate, pioneering clean energy technology, solar panels, and sustainable forestry through debt or equity.

Approaches to impact investing will vary based on a person's goals, values, and means, making it difficult to define broadly. However, there are two key differentiators between impact investing and its philanthropic counterparts:

1. Impact investing is intended to generate returns for the investor.
2. Impact investing has a greater potential for scale because the practice focuses on backing sustainable businesses that

create solutions as a force for good. Business has a greater potential because it can act on so many levels and influence so many different stakeholders—not only customers and employees but also suppliers, the environment, communities in which it operates, and even government if the business is involved in policy.

Impact investing is not just isolated to one asset class. It can be represented across many different asset classes, such as stocks, bonds, and real estate. There are some guidelines as to what does or does not qualify as an impact investment. For instance, some of the tools and language utilized around impact investing include:

- **Environmental, social, and corporate governance (ESG):** Investments screened for these three factors offer a lens through which investments, company operations, and risk factors are viewed. If companies do not meet specific ESG requirements, they can be excluded from an ESG portfolio.

- **Sustainable Development Goals (SDGs):** Leaders at the United Nations unveiled this set of seventeen goals in 2015 in the hopes of creating a more equitable and sustainable world by 2030. These goals are focused on ending poverty, fighting inequality, and addressing climate change. The Sustainable Development Goals serve as reference categories around which investors can design their intended social and environmental impact and envision what is possible.[8]

- **Impact washing:** Impact washing is a term used when a company or organization portrays itself as being purpose-driven or environmentally friendly, but in reality, their efforts are inconsistent at best and disingenuous at worst.

- **B Corporations:** This organizational designation is designed around a concept known as *stakeholder capitalism.* B Corporations pursue a triple-bottom-line strategy, meaning that in addition to pursuing profits, they also pursue benefits for people and for the planet as well.

I will elaborate on each of these concepts and how they relate to impact investing throughout the book. For now, simply understand that the key principle of impact investing is investing in a cause or practice that matters to you and that you see as a force for good.

Impact investing is meant to change the typical approach to investments so that conscious investors can come to greater meaning and purpose. If you are not sure yet what that approach might look like, do not worry. As you begin to shape a new mindset around your impact, you will find more opportunities to invest your resources with greater purpose, including not only finances but time, effort, and connections as well.

CAPITALISM FROM MANY DIMENSIONS

Jessica Droste Yagan, CEO of Impact Engine, an investment firm that manages funds to invest in for-profit, positive-impact businesses, has shaped my understanding of the need for impact investing within our current financial system.

"To me, capitalism has been amazing for a beautiful, elegant system, and [it has] helped align resources," Yagan says.[9] In that way, capitalism has had a positive impact. However, "We haven't demanded enough of it." But, as Yagan says, "The heart of capitalism can work for many different dimensions."

To explain her point, Yagan uses the example of coffee. It used to be that consumers just wanted their coffee to be affordable and to taste good, which is exactly what coffee shops and restaurants provided. Today, however, consumers want to know more. They want to know how their coffee was grown, whether the farmers were paid well, and whether the production of that coffee harmed the environment in any way. When consumers demand it, they often get it.

With impact investing, "There is this opportunity to take this beautiful, efficient system of capitalism and demand more of it," Yagan says. "So, as investors we can say, 'Yes, I want to make money, but also, I demand that you do it in a way that is aligned with my values or that is solving an important problem.'"[10]

This perspective resonated with me. Impact investing is not about tearing down or replacing the current financial system. It is about engaging that system to do *more*—to not only create financial returns but also to create a positive impact in the process. This can include all of the tools available to us, such as starting with making sure your bank is lending your savings account in a way that resonates with you and moving on to your investment portfolio or retirement savings.

IMPACT DOES NOT PRECLUDE PROFIT

While the woman seated next to me at the lunch meeting was enamored right away, I often encounter pushback, especially from asset managers. They might acknowledge that the next generation is open to impact investing, but at the end of the day, they or their clients do not want to give up returns in favor of impact.

These fears stem from a common misconception that impact investing is, in fact, philanthropy by another name.

Once, I sat stunned in an impact investment meeting as someone stood up to talk about his experience. He said, "One day, I wanted to become an impact investor. And I called up my broker and I said, 'Sell everything. I do not care what the markets are doing.' I took a loss on my portfolio, and now, I want to move forward with a clean slate."

I admired this man's intentions, but his actions revealed a lack of strategic thinking. It was not necessarily bad that he sold at a loss. In fact, he probably thought he was justified in doing so. On the whole, the prevailing thought in the asset management industry is that a market downturn (such as during the wild market fluctuations caused by the COVID-19 pandemic in 2020) represents a good opportunity for people to move their portfolios into investments screened for ESG factors. This belief stems from the desire to not pay capital gains taxes for assets sold at a gain, and it is one reason why so many avoided selling their stocks during the 2010s in order to become more active in impact investing.

Overall, this is a sound strategic approach—wait for the markets to drop, sell what you own, and invest in something more impactful.

However, that is not what this person was doing. He sold at a loss purely because he was eager to become an impact investor, and he was less concerned with the financial consequences of that choice.

Let us be clear: financial detriment is not a noble thing to do to yourself. You are not a martyr. Know that aligning your values does not happen overnight, and take your time. Keeping all returns in mind, including financial returns, can yield positive results.

Impact investing is simply investing that asks you to factor in other criteria than financial returns. While there are some exceptions, it generally does not require sacrifice of profit or return. However, experts acknowledge that there are specific social and environmental needs that require subsidy, including specific types of renewable energy generation. These experts largely advocate that the rules of the game need to be changed with regard to how our economy works. I will talk more later in the book about the moral imperative for doing good, how social and environmental factors will continue to play a role in our economy in a greater way in the coming decades, and how these factors should be better integrated into our system of capitalism.[11]

There are certain areas where different types of investing and different stakeholders can contribute in specific ways to solve a social or environmental problem. But in general, there are solutions that can offer financial return and impact, hand in hand.

Impact investing is not a risky, fringe approach to investing. In fact, as the economy shifts away from profit and toward purpose, one in every three dollars under professional management is already invested using socially responsible strategies.[12] Assets held in funds that have been screened for ESG factors have risen by an astounding 142 percent since 2012.

This shift can be seen not only in how people invest but in how they make their purchase decisions as well. Globally, the market of ESG investments is estimated to be $30.7 trillion—and it is growing. As I write this near the end of 2020, emerging research suggests that many variations of impact investing will perform better after the COVID-19 pandemic as investors shift priorities.[13] However, evidence of ESG outperformance was emerging long before the pandemic hit.

In 2019, for instance, one study of 2,800 global stocks by the BlackRock Investment Institute found that ESG portfolios can be more resilient in downturn scenarios—suggesting that factors such as good governance, resilient supply chains, and environmentally sustainable business practices tend to do well in downturns.[14] Humanity's eyes are now being turned to the notion that more than just shareholders are impacted by investments.

Another study, by State Street Global Advisors, found that almost 70 percent of ESG investors stated that these investments helped them manage volatility.[15] ESG practices are also being viewed as risk mitigators in business. Therefore, avoiding companies that do not have good governance, do not have sustainable supply chains, or do not have sound environmental policies will help investment portfolios navigate the future and the risks that could arise in the coming decades. Responsible companies do not just perform the same. In fact, some research suggests they perform better—especially during volatile times. To the conscious investor, this means returns *do not* have to be sacrificed and that, in fact, their ESG compliant invest-ment holdings may provide opportunities for better, more sustain-able returns.

This is not just speculation. Already, investors, who factor in ESG criteria into their investment decision making, have consistently found their investment has paid off. For instance, 80 percent of impact investors report financial and social returns that are in line with their expectations.[16] Further, 15 percent of impact investors report that their impact investments are actually *outperforming* their expectations.[17] The majority of impact investors are exceeding what they hope to earn with their impact investments—and they are ben-efitting from the upside of social and environmental performance at the same time. Finally, a Harvard Business School study across thirty years and forty-eight industries found that businesses integrating social and environmental impact outperform their competitors and make higher-return investments.[18] I wonder if that is because they care about all stakeholders?

Socially and environmentally conscious companies that have produced double-bottom-line returns for decades, like Seventh Generation, are inculcating a new generation of companies—the B Corporation, which is operating in ways that are better for workers, community, customers, and the environment. The company pursues this double-bottom-line strategy in ways both large and small. For instance, Seventh Generation uses only plant-based ingredients, the company does not use any synthetic fragrances or dyes that would harm the environment, and all packaging is recycled. In these and other ways, Seventh Generation works to minimize their impact on people and the planet in making and designing their products. The company also exhibits transparency in their processes and advocates for what the company stands for. The success of companies like Seventh Generation not only makes them a safe investment but a *good* investment.[19]

B Corporations and other entities are examples of a broader movement of the *purpose-driven business*. The purpose-driven business—sometimes referred to as a social enterprise—stands for and takes action on something bigger than just its products and services. It acts for all stakeholders, rather than just shareholders.

The purpose-driven business is closely aligned with the concept of conscious capitalism. In practice, conscious capitalism is dedicated to elevating humanity through business. According to the Conscious Capitalism organization, business leaders that view themselves as part of the conscious capitalism movement focus on having a purpose beyond profit, cultivating their conscious leadership and culture throughout their business. In other words, they prioritize stakeholder orientation as opposed to shareholder primacy.[20]

The purpose-driven business practicing conscious capitalism is focused both on creating positive impact and generating profit. And to the latter point, they have largely succeeded. Many examples exist in the Beyond Capital investment portfolio. By targeting and investing in other purpose-driven businesses, Beyond Capital has created positive financial return while improving the livelihoods of over seven million people (and counting!) as of 2020.

Once you accept that impact and financial return are not mutually exclusive, be careful not to slip back into a solely "finance-first mentality." After all, returns are important but so is impact. The ability to generate strong returns is a feature of impact investing but not the panacea. Making money with no regard for positive social, environmental, tech, and governance outcomes will never be fulfilling and, as many of us have experienced, can never be "enough."

NATASHA'S STORY

In 2012, my good friend and Beyond Capital supporter Natasha Mueller was managing her investment portfolio, when an advisor presented an opportunity to invest in a solar park. Because it contributed to climate change mitigation and helped establish renewable energy as a viable investment strategy, the investment aligned with her values, and she chose to move ahead with it. To this day, that investment has been one of the best performing assets in her portfolio.

That solar park was Natasha's proverbial lightbulb moment as a conscious investor—the catalyst that helped her see the impact her investments could have. At the time, impact investing was only just beginning to attract attention. From that one investment, she was inspired to do more.

Today, Natasha invests in companies that work toward improving global food systems, clean technology, education, the environment, mental health, and gender equality. She aims to be part of systemic change by supporting overlapping sectors of good. For example, food systems affect both the environment and our physical and mental health, and education is critical for creating a productive economic workforce.

Like many millennials, Natasha has a lifelong desire to do good. She worked at the United Nations after completing her college studies and later spent time as an activist and a volunteer. Each stop on this journey reflected her belief that human capital, time, and networks could create impact, and later, she learned that her finances could be used in a similar way. The key is to first understand your values, then back them up with whatever resources you have to create a positive impact.

BEYOND CAPITAL—BOLD FINANCIAL INVESTMENTS

At Beyond Capital, as a venture capital fund, we invest in companies with funding in addition to management advisory and mentoring, all dedicated to the success of the enterprise. Having a clear and unwavering focus on impact drives our decisions on who to invest in as well as what kind of value-added support we will provide.

While seed stage capital is often overlooked by investors, and it is difficult for businesses to access early-stage funding, we find it is the perfect place to contribute to significant positive impact. With a mission to invest in companies that improve the lives of low-income individuals, early startups who can benefit from a range of intensive support often fit the criteria. Rather than functioning as silent financiers, we become their sounding board, their shoulder to cry on, and their long-term partners.

Remarkably, volunteers have driven our model for over a decade. Every year, we galvanize hundreds of thousands of dollars' worth of top talent to help us find the right businesses to invest in and support. In fact, volunteering your time is an excellent start to impact investing, even if you are not ready for financial commitments.

My good friend and executive coach Keren Eldad, whom you will hear more about throughout the book, gives her time every week as a suicide prevention coach on the Crisis Text line. The organization connects trained citizens with individuals who are feeling depressed, scared, or in mental health crisis. Even at a low level of hours, this is a huge emotional and professional commitment, with calls often coming through in the middle of the night when the rest of the United States is sleeping. Yet, the impact of saving a life cannot be effectively quantified.

Scale is embedded in this kind of work, even if its full measure remains unseen. It is an investment of time, which creates significant impact. These are the opportunities that become visible with a shift in perspective toward consciousness and impact.

the economy for good

Every decision comes with positive or negative consequences, and investment decisions are no different. Money is not devoid of emotion or meaning, and when one is cavalier with it, its potential power is lost.

In recent years, business has shifted to become more conscious of personal impact. More leaders now understand that a company's success depends on the emotional connection that its employees have to the work that they are doing.[21] During the COVID-19 pandemic, values came to the forefront of investor, employee, and consumer decision-making—chief among them are the need for disaster preparedness, continuity planning, and paid sick leave for employees working remotely.[22]

This was not the only example of a shift in market and investor behavior that the COVID-19 pandemic helped bring to light. *MarketWatch* speculated that the pandemic had realigned investor priorities around a "new normal of sustainability."[23] During the mass shutdowns in the spring of 2020, many observers noted that the sharp drop in emissions marked a tremendous opportunity for us to make some of our habits and behaviors more permanent in order to keep global warming below the 1.5-degrees Celsius level set in Paris Agreements.[24] Finally, consumer habits changed as well, as analysts noted a dramatic shift toward supporting small or local businesses in the wake of the pandemic. It appears that, in an environment where many businesses are threatened, conscious consumers are choosing to support the businesses that their money can most directly impact.[25]

In truth, the changes brought about by the COVID-19 pandemic may take years for us to sort through and understand. Anecdotally, however, I have certainly seen these larger phenomena at play within the context of our work at Beyond Capital. In 2020, we saw our community grow closer than ever, as those who supported our work became more focused on engaging as a community.

The new, community-oriented, and purpose-driven economy will be defined by the simultaneous pursuit of social and environmental impact and business success. Business will be viewed as a force for good, money will no longer be a taboo subject, and societal and environmental good will be a requirement for corporations rather than a benefit.

For example, many companies were quickly judged on whether they acted according to their values in their response to the COVID-19 pandemic. Just Capital, a research group focused on capitalism that works for all Americans, suggests that companies, at all times, should support workers' health and financial security; adopt practices to minimize job loss; put workers first; support communities, local suppliers, and customers; and have the C-Suite lead by example. To advocate for these behaviors, they implemented a tracker to highlight the efforts of companies leading this charge. This is an open, public tool that anyone can use.[26] [27]

Another excellent resource comes from the Harvard Business Review, which offers a guide on how to promote racial equity in the workplace. This tool serves as a useful framework for leaders to establish problem awareness, root cause analysis, empathy, strategy, and sacrifice as a part of a framework to have a more equitable workplace.[28]

More broadly, there has been another movement toward recognizing businesses for their purpose-driven efforts. Certifications and filing statuses that screen for impact criteria are a start in this direction, but without rewarding the companies that meet the criteria, they are not enough to jump-start the new economy. In that regard, perhaps financial gain offers the greatest incentive. According to one analysis, achieving the Sustainable Development Goals (SDGs) would create a $12 trillion market and create 380 million jobs by 2030.[29]

When the market for conscious investing grows into the potential it has demonstrated thus far—driven by impact investors like Beyond Capital, Natasha, Keren, and you—screening will be a prerequisite for much greater benefits and consequences. Companies will eventually learn that impact criteria gains them access to investments, and *that* is where change can start to happen.

In the meantime, impact investing is a tool that anyone can use in a life marked by purpose, meaning, and fulfillment.

CHAPTER 2

the case for meaning

n 1996, two Canadian entrepreneurs set out to create a business that focused on people, planet, and prosperity. The result was Left Coast Naturals, which started out as a sustainable food bulk business and then began to build out their own brand, Hippie Snacks, which is available in most grocery stores. Today, as a triple-bottom-line business—measuring impact not only in terms of profit but also in people and planet—the same values are at the forefront of the Left Coast Naturals' branding, website, and culture.

Left Coast's CEO, Ian Walker, was just twenty-four when he co-founded the company, and his standards have not wavered since the beginning. As a company, Left Coast Naturals cares *a lot* about the sustainability of their food—using organic farming and sustainable agricultural practices for both consumer health and for the benefit and regeneration of the environment. All of their suppliers commit to strict non-GMO policies and submit to regular audits, and all of their ingredients are heavily researched down to the smallest detail. For example, they have found that trucking honey from Alberta to Canada's west coast is more energy intensive than importing quinoa from Peru. As Walker puts it, their goal is to be "smarter than your average organic food company."[30]

Whenever someone buys products from Left Coast Naturals, they can be sure that the company has done their due diligence and created a product that is good for the body and for the planet. And they have not overlooked their own employees either. The company provides incentives for employees to live a more socially impactful lifestyle. For example, based on research that says organic groceries cost seventy-five dollars more each week, the company gives its employees seventy-five dollars a week to cover the difference if they commit to eating organic. Employees are also incentivized to ride bikes to work and to make environmental improvements to their homes. After more than twenty years in business, Left Coast Naturals has succeeded in their goal to create a company culture that lives and breathes their original mission of people, planet, and prosperity.

While the business is certified as a B Corporation, certifications mean less to the founders than the impact that they hope to create. Walker puts it this way: "I don't want to be the biggest company. I just want to be the most impactful business."

So, what is it that drives a business toward meaning and impact over profit alone? It is the same thing that moves us as individuals. Meaning gives us a reason to wake up in the morning. It makes life exciting. Believe it or not, you can get this same feeling with your work and the way you spend and invest your money.

Conscious investing applies purpose, meaning, and values to money. It is where you regain an emotional connection to money—where your investments "spark joy," as author and lifestyle expert Marie Kondo so beautifully puts it.

Through impact investing, you can consciously break down your detachment to money and bring your spending and investing choices closer into alignment with your values, meaning, and joy, which ultimately drives lasting success.

a generational pursuit of purpose

John Wesley is credited with instructing his Methodist followers, "Do all the good you can, by all the means you can, in all the ways you can, in all the places you can, at all the times you can, to all the people you can, as long as you ever can." From these cherished eighteenth-century instructions to modern B Corporation status and ESG labels, there is an appeal to a meaning-based existence that speaks to us all.

This movement toward conscious uses of wealth will only continue to grow as younger generations wield increasing buying power. Millennials and members of Gen Z demand the integration of social values into every aspect of life, from politics to work to finances. In fact, Fidelity estimates that as much as 77 percent of millennials have already made an impact investment—and this is only the beginning.[31]

Not only do younger investors genuinely care about what is happening around them, but they live in a time where information can be spread at a lightning pace. Further, they famously value experience, meaning, and fulfillment over money, in stark contrast to older generations. Impact has become the norm for younger generations, with many of them unable to remember a time when this was not the case. Not only does this perception drive impact investments, but it also means that Gen Z spends more time questioning just how effective (or ineffective) an impact actually is.

This has led some analysts to characterize Gen Z in particular as a pragmatic generation—one focused not only on making a difference but also on achieving happiness and security both in and outside of work.[32] This may be why members of Gen Z are 55 percent more likely to start a business than millennials.[33] Clearly, this is a generation of highly motivated entrepreneurs, who are not afraid to think outside the box or actively pursue practical and applicable solutions to the issues confronting them.

In this way, current generations reflect the same root desire as John Wesley did nearly three centuries prior. Seeing these groups, who are overwhelmingly driven by both meaning and productivity, I feel a ray of hope for the continuation of social entrepreneurship and the future of our society. Like me, they recognize that no investment is neutral. Money itself might be an amoral tool, but as soon as it is used, some kind of positive or negative outcome is set in motion. Ignorance truly is bliss, for once you realize that a potential investment is inconsistent with your values, it is impossible to reverse that knowledge.

This growing awareness can be seen as the first steps into a practice commonly known as *wealth consciousness*. As Keren Eldad pointed out in the foreword, money is a currency to which investors can assign a positive or negative meaning—which can drive the outcome, as evidenced by looking at where we spend our own money. Wealth consciousness asks us to face that reality in pursuit of the benefits that await on the other side. Most importantly, it asks us to come to the realization that members of Gen Z are born into: money without purpose will never be enough.

According to Shawn Achor, an author, researcher, and advocate for positive psychology, the moving target of success is only stopped by meaning—and only meaning can bring success. To illustrate what he means, Achor points to what he calls the "happiness advantage." Research has shown that people with a positive mindset perform better in the face of challenge, which in turn correlates to better business outcomes.[34] This should not come as a big surprise. After all, as Brother David Steindl-Rast says, all of us *want* to be happy.[35] The key is understanding what you can do to create that happiness.

Boomers learned it was not profit. Gen X decided it was not in hustle and grind. Millennials got closer to the mark, and Gen Z seem to have it all together. The question is whether to stay the course dictated by society at large or become conscious of the impact, meaning, and ultimate joy that our financial choices can bring. Will they use impact investing to apply the happiness advantage to our money, or will they protect the taboo?

looking for *saral jeevan*

In late 2019, I traveled with fifteen other members of the Beyond Capital team and board to India, so that we could meet face-to-face with the management teams of our portfolio companies. This was not an easy trip. My fellow travelers and I were pushed well beyond our comfort zone in long car rides and packed daily schedules, with most of that time spent on the road, making it impossible to get the kind of rest we were accustomed to. And yet, if I only had one word to describe the experience, it would be *gratitude.*

The pivotal moment came when we met with the women driving the sales at Frontier Markets, a business that provides access to basic goods and services in the rural "last mile"—the end point of access. These are areas so remote, they are untouched by the commercial markets we eat, sleep, and breathe in developed countries. The company's name for its salesforce—*Saral Jeevan Sahelis,* or "easy life, friends"—is simple but powerful.

Hina is twenty-six and stands at just over five feet tall, but her chin was held high as she led us to one of her customers. She lives in a small village a couple of hours outside of Delhi, one of many of its kind that Frontier Markets serves.

Frontier Markets employs over 3,800 women as *Saral Jeevan Sahelis* who work hard to provide for their families. The women we met told us how they save their earnings for important life events we can relate to, such as a child's marriage, as well as needs we sometimes take for granted, such as education or a household washing machine. And their efforts were paying off. Both their lives and their social standing had improved since Frontier Markets had grown as a company. Their husbands and families were proud of them, and Hina's bold stroll through the main road of her village demonstrated her elevated standing in the community. The company has also generated positive financial results and developed a market that not many big companies can reach. I am excited by the financial return potential for this investment as well.

I walked away grateful for each moment of that experience— grateful for the choice we made to support Frontier Markets, grateful for the choices we have here in our lives, and grateful for the possibility of contributing beyond myself.

Saral Jeevan might be different for everyone, but we are all in pursuit of it. Gratitude for what ease we do have often becomes clearer as we share experiences, time, and resources with others. According to Brother Steindl-Rast, this is the secret ingredient to happiness.

GRATITUDE AS A CORNERSTONE OF MEANING

At Beyond Capital, we have invested in rural health clinics that solve the major problem of access to primary care in remote areas. On that trip to India, I also spent time on the ground visiting our investment in Karma Healthcare, a telemedicine healthcare company whose story I will share throughout this book. My strong belief and support of that company in particular stems from my gratitude for healthcare access when my son's life was on the line.

Just three weeks after he was born, my son, Alessandro, contracted a bacterial infection that sent us rushing to Cedars Sinai hospital in

Los Angeles on a Sunday afternoon. In spite of the chaos and sleep deprivation of having a new baby, my husband had noticed our son was breathing heavily, and soon after, he spiked a fever. As soon as we arrived, he was in immediate triage in the emergency room. In the hours that followed, doctors had to restart his heart, administer the strongest panel of antibiotics and antiviral medicine available, and perform a spinal tap.

Thirty-six hours later, my tiny infant son had been released from the ICU with a catheter administering antibiotics to his heart and was recovering well. He would stay in the hospital for another ten days, then go home to grow into a rambunctious, curious, wonderful little boy.

It is difficult to recount that experience without tears: my son beat the odds of his infection, with no lasting side effects. Despite the stress and worry inherent in those memories, the strongest feeling that I ever remember from this experience is gratitude for the access to healthcare that was literally at my fingertips and in close proximity.

Gratitude has fueled over a decade of inspiration and enthusiasm for the work I am able to do, and gratitude in moments like these has inspired further investments for related causes.

In your own pursuit of inspiration, enthusiasm, and meaning, remember that it is not the circumstance that is most important but your perspective. The more you pursue gratitude in your life, the more you find it—and, therefore, the more you enrich your life.

AJAITA'S STORY

My close friend, Ajaita Shah, has worked for over a decade as a social entrepreneur in India. Her current business, Frontier Markets, which is part of the Beyond Capital portfolio, distributes consumer durables and essentials, including renewable energy products like solar lanterns to people who mostly live below the poverty line. The company has reached over four million individuals, selling over eight hundred thousand products as of 2020.

But as a purpose-driven leader, she went one step further: she created a specific component in her business model that brought local women in as members of her sales force.

She is constantly thinking about women in Rajasthan, a place where women are second-class citizens. While Shah could have distributed her products through local shops typically run by men, she quickly saw the social impact victory that came from engaging rural women as *Saral Jeevan Sahelis* with deep networks, which could help distribute more renewable energy and consumer products in their local communities. Over ten thousand women have been employed by the company. These women have directly informed the growth of Frontier Markets.

enlightened self-interest

How can we all thrive together? Can we create abundance for everyone, and if so, how do we make that a reality? While we may not actually have a sense of security and many will still lack access to critical goods and services, viewing progress as a zero-sum game where the pie is finite puts everyone only into survival mode.

According to entrepreneur Dan Price, founder and CEO of Gravity Payments, the answer is through a mindset known as *enlightened self-interest*. When a person acts to further the interests of others, ultimately those actions serve their own self-interests.

It is easy to get trapped in the mindset that the pie is finite, that there are only so many resources to go around for everyone. It is from this mindset billionaires are praised for giving their money to charitable causes, even though it is often not the most effective means of helping those who are socioeconomically disadvantaged. Further, many believe that giving or helping others—whether through welfare, reparations, or affirmative action, for instance—means there will be fewer resources and opportunities for us.

In fact, research has shown the opposite is true. When you work to elevate the standards for everyone, you see positive benefits for yourself and for society. For instance, research has found that helping others not only produces emotional satisfaction and a sense of purpose, but it also reduces stress and tension and boosts heart health.[36] Other studies have shown that kindness has a compounding effect. When we are kind to others, they are far more likely to pay that kindness forward.[37] It is perhaps no surprise, then, that helping others not only benefits us and those we assist but also society at large. According to a 2018 World Bank study, social safety nets—programs designed specifically with the intention of helping others—not only help to elevate individuals, families, and communities out of poverty but also help to reduce inequality. And in a society where everyone is on more equal ground, everyone benefits.[38]

These concepts are at the core of *servant leadership*, a leadership philosophy in which the goal is to serve others. It encompasses self-awareness, humility, integrity, foresight, listening, trusting, being collaborative, resolving conflicts, not abusing authority, and being results-oriented. It is from this philosophy that Price made the controversial decision to provide a minimum $70,000 salary to all his employees at Gravity Payments, which resulted in a cut to his own salary. As someone in a position of influence with resources, Price sought to elevate the standards for everyone within his organization, not just himself.

While this decision may have raised some eyebrows, it was consistent with Price's mission. Price first got the idea for Gravity Payments after a hearing about the exorbitant fees his friend's coffee shop was paying just to process credit cards. Price strongly believed that small businesses were very important for the American economy—so important, in fact, that he became focused on creating a payment processing solution that would help them thrive.

By 2015, Gravity had grown to rival Visa and Mastercard in its capabilities. By that time, however, Price had shifted his focus to another problem that many small businesses faced: paying their employees a decent wage. Price was alarmed by the statistics he read, which indicated that while productivity had risen by 70 percent of the past forty years, worker pay had only increased by 11.6 percent during that same time. So, he decided to cut his own salary and start all his employees at $70,000 a year.

This choice made Price a bit of a CEO activist. Some praised his decision, while others saw it as a stunt that would eventually bankrupt the company. To Price, because he was so focused on doing the right thing by his employees, there was no other choice. As Price put it, "When I announced I was taking a $1 million pay cut to pay everyone $70,000 a year, the situation was that I was now in a community where everybody could meet their needs. And Gravity Payments became more about the people and the principles behind the company."

Price is still an owner of his business—he did not "sell it all" or otherwise give it all away. Price firmly believes that by providing what he considered a living wage to his employees that he was enriching his community and, therefore, enriching his own life.[39] From this perspective, contributing beyond yourself is about more than simply feeling good. It is also critical to your success and the success of those around you. If you want to further your own position, then you have a duty to do good in society.

One application of enlightened self-interest for entrepreneurs and business owners is to follow the same path as Price and build a company around this sense of duty. Through your business, you can improve the lives of everyone your business touches—including your own. Such an approach is not as far away as you might think. In fact, as Price's story illustrates, in some ways it is already here. Businesses and investors are already acting from a perspective of enlightened self-interest, and they have the success stories to validate this approach and bring it to the mainstream. As a conscious investor, you can implement the same principles Price and Shah employ in your investments, and with the other choices embedded in all your resources.

This is a major driver of conscious investing, the desire to know that society is flourishing for everyone and that others' success is meaningful to the health and well-being of you and your family. While this concept may seem abstract at first, ask yourself: How much do you want the neighborhoods adjacent to your own to be struggling? How much do you want the public schools in your area to be underfunded? Most likely, not at all.

Ultimately, enlightened self-interest is equivalent to a wealth consciousness of abundance. Just as acting in a mindset of enlightened self-interest is shown to have positive benefits for all, acting in a mindset of only self-interest has the opposite effect. Both in the financial crisis of 2008 and the corresponding recession that resulted from the COVID-19 pandemic of 2020, societies across the globe saw firsthand how inequality for some led to a crisis that could touch all sectors of the economy. As my coach Keren Eldad often says, we are all in this together.

the CEO mindset

My husband, Hooman, is an extremely accomplished CEO who has run billion-dollar businesses in the past. He and I started Beyond Capital together to use our skills and networks for good, and he is always excited to share his philosophy of what he calls The CEO Mindset with our donors, volunteers, and the businesses we invest in. The qualities of The CEO Mindset are exemplified by the conscious leaders described throughout this book, but the same qualities can extend to how we view our investments. For Hooman, our work at Beyond Capital helped to inform his thinking around this concept.

The CEO Mindset is a way of running your life by using certain business skills, which often means something very different than the stern authority that most of us associate with high-powered leadership. Instead, the most effective leader has qualities such as decisiveness, adaptability, and consistency—and, most importantly, surrounding yourself with the greatest people and making a contribution beyond yourself. These skills are vitally important, whether you are running a global business, a nonprofit, or a household.

Bill and Melinda Gates are an excellent example of reaching out beyond themselves, becoming involved in polio eradication, rethinking our nuclear energy resources, and creating new forms of toilets in the developing world. Not only are they willing to contribute beyond themselves, but they are also willing to take risks in favor of solutions. Bill and Melinda Gates apply entrepreneurial approaches to solving everyday problems for individuals and communities across the globe.

When I think of Bill and Melinda Gates as role models, it is not for their wealth but for their model of doing good with the money they have made. I am proud to think that Hooman and I have very similar approaches to investments, wanting to use our skills and resources to do good. It is not about what resources you have but rather what mindset you approach them with. A CEO Mindset with a solutions-oriented approach to the issues you are passionate about can create exponential change.

NINE PILLARS OF THE CEO MINDSET

1. **Create your vision.** Live it and communicate it and let yourself be guided by your vision.

2. **Be inspiring.** Unite stakeholders around a common purpose. Be observant, empathetic, and listen. Build a great company culture, nurture safety, share risk, and unite around a common purpose. Mistakes are not failures—allow for vulnerability.

3. **Be adaptable and consistently learning.** Be prepared. As a leader, you must always be a student. Stay curious, sharpen your tools, seek out new skills, and do not get discouraged when you fail!

4. **Be decisive.** Make fewer decisions: focus on what is important and delegate appropriately. Do not worry about being perfect: move forward and continually improve.

5. **Be reliable.** Be on time, respect deadlines, and honor consistency.

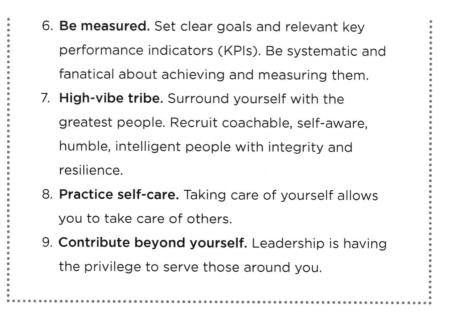

6. **Be measured.** Set clear goals and relevant key performance indicators (KPIs). Be systematic and fanatical about achieving and measuring them.

7. **High-vibe tribe.** Surround yourself with the greatest people. Recruit coachable, self-aware, humble, intelligent people with integrity and resilience.

8. **Practice self-care.** Taking care of yourself allows you to take care of others.

9. **Contribute beyond yourself.** Leadership is having the privilege to serve those around you.

I believe leaders are made, not born. If you heed these nine principles of effective leadership, you will come closer to achieving the success you seek—and by necessity, this includes contributing beyond yourself.

Here is the ultimate truth: people are happiest when they are giving. For instance, think about how you felt during the COVID-19 pandemic when you were sheltering in place or on lockdown. You may have felt a strong desire to contribute beyond yourself, even if you were unsure how you could. The longer this shutdown played out, the more heartwarming stories emerged of individuals selflessly helping others to make sure everyone could weather the pandemic together.

Unfortunately, the inverse also occurred as well, with both local and world leaders choosing to ignore the clear needs of others in favor of their own greed, selfishness, or perhaps insecurity. These leaders stand in sharp contrast to those who seek to understand the diverse perspectives of others and who sow seeds of benefit for others around them in order to reap a harvest of support. Leaders excel when they invest in the development of their teams because they realize they can do more with others than they can on their own.

When Hooman and I founded Beyond Capital in 2009, I never dreamed of reaching over seven million people—and on our own, we could never have made it happen. Together with the contributors, leaders, and role players involved, our impact is limitless. No amount of wealth or personal success could compare to the happiness and fulfillment found in that realization.

This feeling reflects what author Brené Brown would describe as *wholeheartedness*. In her book, *Dare to Lead*, Brown defines wholeheartedness as capturing the essence of a fully examined emotional life and a liberated heart. Put another way, she sees wholeheartedness as the process of integrating our thinking, feeling, and behavior. To drive her point home even further, she points out that the Latin root of "integrate" is intregrare, or "to make whole."

Brown has been an outspoken advocate of wholeheartedness because, in her experience, she has found it missing from the leadership and culture of most modern companies. As Brown says, "Leaders still subscribe to this myth that if we sever the heart from our work, we will be more productive, efficient, and easier to manage." The problem, she says, is that: "When we imprison the heart, we kill courage, losing control."[40]

This zero-sum thinking is a symptom of the belief that good for others cannot be good for the individual. Unfortunately, this is precisely how many leaders currently think—and, frankly, what holds individuals back from pursuing impact investing.

As a result, the concept of wholeheartedness has remained largely absent in the business conversation—and its absence has poisoned the way our leaders think about capitalism and conduct their businesses. By not acknowledging that a wholehearted approach to capitalism is possible, these leaders are precluding the ability to do good with their business activities and setting an example that purpose cannot be found in money.

During my early career on Wall Street, I experienced firsthand what it feels like when your heart is absent from your work. It was hard to find a true authentic connection to my work when making money was the ultimate goal and feelings were largely absent from the conversation, even though I loved my up-and-coming career. While the founder of my firm was socially minded and implemented diversity in the workplace, I can see now how our investments could have better integrated with their social and environmental qualities rather than being chiefly concerned with profit and letting client demands lead our strategy.

If you speak to many of the women who have worked on Wall Street, they will tell you that they had to work harder to overcome bias and were expected to act like their male counterparts. I personally also felt that female mentorship was lacking, except for the incredible CFO of our firm, who instilled a lifelong confidence in me that my drive would lead to success. However, what impacted me the most was not just how miserable it is to work in an industry that has perpetuated a return-first status quo for decades but how long it takes to overcome the effect that can have on your mindset. In fact, it took me over a decade to truly understand that investing does not have to be a zero-sum game and that money being paramount will not drive my personal happiness and success.

Impact investing has always been important to me, but if I am being fully transparent, I have not always approached it from the heart. I wanted to, but I could not. I was hardened by my experience in finance and within a culture where I was told that my feelings did not matter and should not be considered in my investment decisions. When I started Beyond Capital, I worked hard to implement The CEO Mindset leadership qualities into our work. Setting a vision that would acknowledge the opportunity for investing with positive impact in mind, assembling a team that enabled me to act from a place of deep inspiration, and together, setting goals—all while acknowledging my many roles as a CEO, mother, wife, friend, family member, and citizen. The result was a clear ability to find success in contributing beyond myself, whether my contribution was small or large.

From time to time, I still meet finance professionals lacking the drive to consider more than the financial return potential of investments or simply ignoring the fact that investments can have other types of impacts and returns. I have written this book in part to tell you that if you have ever felt this way too, it is not too late. It may take time, but you *can* move back to that feeling of being connected to the solution.

a framework for reimagining capitalism

In her book *Reimagining Capitalism in a World on Fire*, Harvard Business School Professor Rebecca Henderson paints a fascinating picture of modern capitalism and economics. According to Henderson, over 50 percent of her current students believe that capitalism is broken and that it is not working for them.

These Harvard students may be right. As Henderson argues in her book, a healthy society rests on three legs: a fair and free market, a democratically elected and capable government, and a strong civil society, as reflected by an independent media and a strong voice for labor and employees. Modern American society, says Henderson, has become imbalanced, as business interests have increasingly come to overpower these critical elements.

To help restore balance, Henderson proposes the following steps:

- Create shared value by investing in purpose-driven businesses
- Collaborate rather than compete
- Sit down with professionals in finance, and rewire the system
- Rebuild government
- Press for policies that change people's lives

That is a big job. However, as a result of the threat posed by both global climate change and then COVID-19, Henderson sees an entry point to begin having some of these tough conversations with business leaders as they continue to expose just how dangerous inequality and structural racism are.

The bottom line, Henderson argues, is that concerned citizens can no longer sit still, complain that government is inefficient, and then write it off. As Henderson puts it, "We are pebbles; pebbles start avalanches, and we need a landslide."[41]

The question is, once these conversations have begun, what comes next? How does one reimagine capitalism, to use Henderson's terms—and *why* is it so important to do so?

To answer those questions, we must begin by asking ourselves what our vision of the future looks like—not only as individuals but as a society as a whole. What have we lost when we think about the future? What will a more equitable society look like? What happens when we move away from a more individualistic view on power to a more collective one?

Rebuilding government, for instance, is not just about removing those elected officials deemed unsavory, out of touch, or even destructive. Instead, it is about finding ways to change the very fabric of government and to embrace humanity's power to unite under a shared sense of compassion.

This mindset applies to all of Henderson's action points. What would it look like to reorganize business to include a sense of purpose rather than the "work, work, work" mindset that has come to be the norm? What does your life look like when family and fun go hand in hand, and you know that those around you are not struggling?

Again, the COVID-19 pandemic brought these questions to the forefront of our consciousness. It gave more clarity on the inequities and the systemic patterns holding so many groups back. Further, it showed that many still lacked education on concepts such as systemic inequality and the oneness of humankind and that what happens in one country can impact the whole planet and have a wide reach into the fabric of a society. Achieving progress, then, means linking the interests of the individual to those of society and to encourage everyone to contribute to a global civilization.

how giving fuels success

In his book, *Winners Take All*, Anand Giridharadas explains that money is the best way for philanthropists to make their mark. Unfortunately, this often leads to institutions that worsen problems rather than find solutions. At first, I found Giridharadas's perspective harsh and judgmental, but throughout 2020, I realized the deep importance of his message and understood it comes from a desire to unify.

The premise of Giridharadas's work is that, all too often, society relies on billionaires to donate money to positive social causes. The problem here is that the extremely wealthy notoriously do not represent populations in need (in background, race, or the challenges they face), and they do not always understand what they are donating money toward in the first place.

Winners Take All offers a skeptical view on philanthropy and the good economy, asking us to rethink charitable giving. However, money is not the only vehicle for giving. My husband, Hooman, and I have always considered financial investments extremely important, but we also want to make sure that as investors we foster the right relationships with the companies we are supporting at Beyond

Capital. We are constantly evaluating companies to decide which ones would make a good fit for the portfolio. In 2010, we decided to recruit post-MBAs as one-year volunteers to use their skills to help us find the most legitimate and viable social enterprises to invest in at Beyond Capital.

We quickly realized that people are looking for *more* purpose in their lives, not less, if the additions are fulfilling and meaningful. Despite having countless other responsibilities, those individuals were willing to give their time to us because Beyond Capital was aligned with their personal values.

The time I have spent running Beyond Capital has never felt like work. Yes, I put in considerable effort to stretch beyond my comfort levels and succeed. However, I do it all in service of something that I love, which is why I have been happy to work pro bono to get our work off the ground.

Our chief investment officer, director of due diligence and analysis, and director of social impact all share the same commitment. They all hold advanced degrees. These extremely smart, high-achieving individuals actively *want* to give back their time.[42]

YOGA OFF THE MAT

For over a decade, I have been engaged in meaningful work. I have always been working very hard, but it has never felt like effort. It has taken time to understand the "why" behind what I do, the element that makes my career feel so freeing and effortless. It is a connection to something more than myself—which is realized through impact investing.

This realization might not have ever come if it was not for one of my other passions: yoga. While training for my certification as a yoga instructor, I was told to apply yoga to my life off the mat, as well as on it, to find true spiritual fulfillment. I did not truly understand what that meant until I began to think about how practicing yoga off the mat is a form of practicing service—just as impact investing has become for me.

This realization changed the way I view both my work and every decision in my life.

Although I do not physically practice yoga every day, there is always an element of yoga in whatever I do. When I am in service of others, I am a happy, healthy, fulfilled individual. When I experience hard times, which are inevitable, I find them easier to navigate because of my overriding sense of purpose and gratitude.

The Power of Experience

In 2017, I was introduced to Phil, who had spent decades working in private equity. At the time, he was on the verge of going back to

Harvard University to complete a graduate program on social entre-preneurship, so he could transition his career to be more purpose ori-ented. This man was motivated by the desire to use his finance skills to have a social impact. When we met, we discussed the possibility of him working for one of my portfolio companies. He said, "I would love to give my time and skills for free and pay for my expenses. I just want to gain experience on the ground."

After that conversation, we installed Phil into Karma Healthcare, where he spent two weeks working on the ground as an interim COO. As mentioned in the previous chapter, the goal of Karma is to provide telemedicine for communities in rural areas of India without physical access to doctors. The medical consultations over Karma's proprietary video communication technology reach people who would otherwise be unable to access quality and affordable hos-pitals and doctors, or who otherwise cannot see a specialist in their local area even when very ill.

It is important to note here that Phil had never been to India before, and he volunteered to go to Rajasthan in the month of April, when the temperature was over 100 degrees Fahrenheit, with no air conditioning. As a result, this trip required an extreme context shift for him—both mentally and physically—but that is exactly what he was looking for.

While in Udaipur, India—a beautiful city with a large lake at its center—the CEO of Karma, Jagdeep Gambhir, connected Phil with the local hotel, owned by a friend of his family, as a way to show respect and appreciation for Phil's commitment. Halfway through the volunteer arrangement, I went to check in with both Jagdeep and Phil. Since he was lacking local context, I was not sure what the outcome would be. Fortunately, they were getting on so well that during the entire three or four hours we spent in the car together visiting the clinics, time flew and I literally could not get a word in edgewise.

During those two weeks, Phil rolled up his sleeves and delved into the data. He became a real sounding board to Jagdeep, and according to the feedback we received, his presence was transformative for the company. He also helped them consider their profitability in the long term. Overall, this engagement was a win-win between Phil and Karma Healthcare. The company received valuable support, and Phil gained experience and was in service as a leader.

Of course, contributing beyond yourself does not mean you have to put yourself second or work for free. It is not just about doing good so that you can feel good about yourself. The philosophy of enlightened self-interest states that the person who acts to further the interest of others ultimately serves their own interest. In that way, contributing beyond yourself is critical to both your own success and the success of those around you.[43] It may be our duty to do good in society, but you can do that in a variety of ways, from volunteering to building a business around your desire to do good. The goal may be to improve the lives of everyone affected, but there are many paths you can take to get there.

At Beyond Capital, our desire to do good is in the name. By going *beyond* just capital, we provide more than money to the companies we invest in. We are very aware that companies need access to high-quality services and mentorship to get off the ground, including pro bono legal support and financial modeling assistance, which has executives on the ground helping employees think through critical day-to-day issues.

Through our work, we have impacted the lives of over seven million people—and through only a dozen investments. However, what sticks with me are not the sheer numbers but rather the individual stories of those we have helped. After visits on the ground with companies like ERC Eyecare that provides affordable, on-demand eye care, we hear about individuals like Guna, who lost his left eye as a child but grew up to take over his family business. When an infection impacted the sight in his healthy eye at the age of thirty-five, he could not see or work at all. Because he had access to one of the eye care clinics we had invested in, he was able to obtain the care and glasses he needed to get back to work.

Both metrics and stories matter, reminding us how the most basic goods and services can have significant impact. From the CEO of a groundbreaking health tech company gaining the support he needs to thrive to the individuals his company helps, every dollar, volunteer hour, and resource spent in service of others changes lives for the better. It is not about the budget you have available but how you spend it. As Michael Vlerick, a philosopher of science, author, and global public speaker, says, "I believe that when we have the possibility to change the world for the better, and we all have in some way or another, it is our responsibility to do so."[44]

Many of us are driven to do something more purposeful in our lives, especially today. For some, that means going to a country for the first time to lend your skills for the benefit of others who you have never met. For others, like Jagdeep or Shah, it means starting and leading a purpose-driven business.

If you are part of a generation that has struggled to name your purpose and connect money to meaning, be encouraged that the work you are doing *is* important—not only for the benefit of others but for your happiness and success as well. As you become more conscious about your investment choices, it presents a tremendous opportunity to remove this stigma for others. In the next chapter, I will explain why each of us has a moral obligation to serve, do good, and create a healthier relationship with the purpose of money for the next generations.

CHAPTER 3

the moral imperative for doing good

n his book, *The Life You Can Save*, moral philosopher Peter Singer proposes a hypothetical situation to force consciousness around your perspective of poverty. The situation goes something like this: imagine you are witnessing a child drowning in a lake. Would anything stop you from jumping in to save them? (What if you had not been swimming for a few years? What if you did not know who the child was? What if you were wearing an expensive pair of shoes?)

In Singer's opinion, the answer should always be an emphatic, "No"—nothing would distract you from your instincts to help that child. However, in our daily lives, we often make choices that run counter to our altruistic instincts, even if we are not aware it is happening. We prioritize the proverbial expensive pair of shoes over the potential impact we could have by acting.

None of us means to do this, of course. But to counter this impulse, at least in terms of impact investing, we need to understand just how great our potential impact is.

There are many places where people's lives are hamstrung by issues that they consider trivial in context of their day-to-day lives and choices. To be more specific, they are unable to make purchases that will improve their livelihoods immediately, that amount to no more than the cost of a pair of shoes. Sometimes, this is a purchase; in other cases, it is working capital to grow a small business. The good news is that the small choices we make, whether with our words or with our money, can help others a great deal.

When I think about the difference small choices can make in my own life, one experience stands out in particular. Like many who grew up in New York City, I observed my fellow New Yorkers' tendency to not greet people or even look at them as I went about my day.

This behavior has little to do with class, race, or anything else. More fundamentally, it springs from the fact that New Yorkers are surrounded by a tidal wave of humanity all throughout the day. In these constant, sometimes claustrophobic situations, many learn to turn themselves off, in a sense, to social interaction with strangers.

Early in my career, when I was working in finance, I was also focused on practicing meditation and mindfulness through yoga. One weekend, I was headed home from class when I stopped by a

Duane Reade pharmacy to pick something up. As I was checking out, I made it a point to look at the clerk in the eye and thank him.

"Wow," he said. "You are the first person who has looked me in the eyes all day long."

Years later, I still have not forgotten about that exchange. In fact, that seemingly small moment has come to represent a key tenet of impact investing: understanding all who are involved in our decisions, our money, our time, and our energy. I could have just transacted with the clerk, taken my bottle of water, and left without ever realizing who that person was—a human being.

In this chapter, we are going to discuss what I consider the moral imperative for doing good. As you read through this part of the book, here is the challenge I put to you: Do you want to live with your money and resources only working for those in your immediate circles? Or do you want to create more moments like the one I had with the clerk—to look all your stakeholders in the eye (whether literally or figuratively), to know not just what you are investing in but also what your impact is with those investments?

society depends on cooperation

In late 2019, I attended a talk where Michael Vlerick discussed his book, *The Second Estrangement*. Vlerick is a professor, economist, philosopher, and historian, who lectures on the philosophy of science at the Netherlands' Tilburg University—and his work centers on the philosophical implications of the theory of evolution and how it affects society today.

Vlericks's primary argument is that while we live in a global society, our psychology and institutions lag behind. He walked us through humankind's development of agriculture thousands of years ago and the idea that working on land has led to a largely sedentary lifestyle. Because humans were able to raise animals, they could consume more calories. As the sizes of groups expanded, they became too large for cooperation and humans no longer had to be hunter-gatherers. Vlerick argues that humans are intended to live in groups of one hundred or less, and that living in larger groups leads to tribalism—that is, people voluntarily separate into smaller groups based on self-selected traits (e.g., cultural, religious, racial, etc.).

In the past, he explained, tensions resulting from tribalism have led to the Crusades and other significant geopolitical and cultural conflicts. Today, one way these conflicts manifest is through nationalism, where certain individuals see themselves as distinct from others instead of all being "humans on this one fascinating planet." This is problematic, Vlerick argues, because what separates us from the animals—what makes us special as humans—is that we cooperate with one another.[45]

Achieving progress in a modern sense means linking the interests of the individual to those of the society. Sure, businesses are bound to compete, but they can also cooperate in a way that serves not just shareholders but stakeholders. This concept became even more important during the COVID-19 pandemic, where the true effects of globalization were felt in ways never before seen. In one way or another, everyone is affected by global events. I have believed that this was the case with climate change causing refugee migrations and war. In the spring of 2020, I had the opportunity to ask Vlerick how the COVID-19 pandemic had affected his own views:

> Faced with the current global pandemic, we need to cooperate globally to develop treatments, medicines, and vaccines and—once the pandemic is under control—to recover from the global recession following in its wake. Our tribalistic tendencies ("own group first"), however, are tenacious. Nations bicker over medicines and protective masks and point accusing fingers at each other. But a global crisis of this magnitude has the potential to foster global solidarity. If we manage to join forces, this could be a turning point in our fight against this other global challenge: climate change. Crises are times of rapid change, let's hope we change in the right direction. We must realize that how we react to the COVID-19 pandemic transcends the current crisis.[46]

Even in the face of tremendous tragedy and hardship, there is always opportunity to foster global solidarity. There is hope. There is the potential to emerge from a crisis into a better world. Conscious investing—active engagement in how you spend your time and money—can play a significant role in that.

This process must be undertaken intentionally. The COVID-19 pandemic has harmed almost every aspect of human activity, including conscious and impact investing. During the pandemic, through the Paycheck Protection Program (PPP), banks prioritized existing clients with a credit relationship, leaving out a lot of small businesses and organizations engaged in impactful activities. Large banks were also the first providers of loans, while most banks catering to small businesses came second and only then funded more locally. Although the program was replenished, there was still a knowledge barrier to apply. Further, social impact in the United States has always been driven in large part by Community Development Financial Institutions (CDFIs), which lend to small businesses, schools, health facilities, and affordable housing projects. During the COVID-19 pandemic, these institutions did not provide nearly the same level of support, which in turn put these organizations under tremendous pressure to simply exist, often struggling to pay back their creditors.[47]

This makes impact investors' universe of investments narrow. In order to prove that financial, social, and environmental return can exist hand in hand and to deliver that to their investors, they need to have a healthy ecosystem of companies to invest in. By creating inequities in how small businesses and organizations access relief capital for the global pandemic, it created challenges but also opportunities.

As the Impact Investing Alliance's Fran Seegull notes, this has serious implications for what the economic landscape will look like as society and economies build back better from the COVID-19 pandemic—particularly as it pertains to income inequality. According to Seegull, the global recovery from the 2008 financial crisis was very uneven. The coasts recovered, but the jobs did not come back to low-income communities, and there was a huge level of poverty created and, thereby, a need for affordable housing. In her work with the Impact Investing Alliance, Seegull believes this crisis is an opportunity for us to consider some of the systematic faults that have made us so vulnerable to the virus.

What is important here is not whose fault these inequalities were (no single person or entity can be held entirely at fault), but that we—investors, businesses, and capital markets—have an *opportunity* to take our role in society more seriously and work toward creating a more equitable world. Instead of saying that circumstances will change or that they *could* change, the first thing is that we recognize that they *need* to change. Stepping back to think about the origins of the challenges we face allows us to come to better solutions. If Michael Vlerick's theories hold true, humans struggle so much along political and cultural lines because they were built for a different type of society. His suggestions are threefold: focus on education, promote positive contact between different groups, and insist on women's rights. While there are many ways to go about ameliorating the many issues modern society faces, conscious investing may be the most effective way to cover all three of those approaches at once.

money as a medium for meaning

In spite of talk of tribalism and war, human nature is inherently good. At the heart of it all, we are all looking for happiness, ease, and connection—whether in our personal or our professional lives.

In his book, *Payoff: The Hidden Logic That Shapes Our Motivations*, renowned economist and behavioral economics and psychology professor Dan Ariely describes the results of a study in which he measured which factors drive employees to work hard. According to his findings, employees were not driven by bonuses, healthcare, or even foosball tables. Instead, they were driven by trust, purpose, meaning, mission, and emotional connection. The study evaluated companies on eighty different variables, and the results showed that companies in the S&P 500 Index outperform when their non-financial indicators (happiness and employee engagement, for example) are present and positive.[48]

Humans are ultimately looking for emotional connection. Regardless of what they are doing, they value the mission and seek inspiration from the work.

Conversely, an abundance of scientific and psychological research says that the greater an individual's wealth, the less likely they are to be happy. Specifically, as one study found, the more money a person has, the less generous that person is likely to be. As we discussed earlier, behaviors such as giving and assistance are directly correlated to happiness. The greedier and stingier someone becomes, the less likely that person is to exhibit and perform the very traits and behaviors that lead to happiness.[49]

The harsh reality is that money does not directly correlate to happiness. Perhaps this is why generations before us chose not to speak about money. Without a connection to meaning and purpose, it is not a happy subject—and, therefore, not one perceived to be for children, women, or friends to engage in. For this exact reason, it is important for conscious investing to help turn this tide. All research points to the improvements that can be made with a positive mindset, especially regarding business outcomes.

Capitalism conditions us to believe that wealth is only related to financial prosperity. With a conscious investing mindset, money becomes about more than a financial return. It becomes an opportunity to connect with your money and what you do with it—to cooperate with your fellow humans and regain a sense of humanity. Conscious investing becomes the vehicle that allows you to travel toward emotional connection.

the greatness we can achieve

If a lifelong investor asked me why they should get involved in conscious investing, I would present it as a market opportunity. At Beyond Capital, for instance, impact investing is a chance to become exposed to a new level of rural access—to people who are disconnected from resources and, therefore, brand new to the global market for investment. This same thinking can be applied to many other investments where other social and environmental considerations are taken into account. To be clear, there is a significant opportunity in the impact investing market, which has shown strong compounded annual growth since 2016.[50] Based on a database of over 1,720 impact investors compiled by the Global Impact Investing Network (GIIN) in their Annual Impact Investor Survey, aggregate assets under management for repeat respondents were $98 billion versus $52 billion in 2016.[51]

While I focus throughout this book on sharing the investment case for the regions and sectors I primarily invest in, I encourage you to understand how the areas that you are passionate about can allow for financial return and positive impact progress that fits your goals. For example, investing in climate change solutions and the technological change that will follow is often thought to go hand in hand with the fourth industrial revolution, which will create $26 trillion in market value.[52]

A study called *The Next 4 Billion* examines how large populations in growing countries—earning less than four dollars a day—often do have a budget to afford healthcare, energy access, and agricultural tools and other basic goods and services that will make their lives better.[53] While individually they have a very small amount to spend, together they represent a $5 trillion global market. Thanks to rapid development of the internet and technology, those people are more accessible than ever before.

Over the past decade, I have watched as business models that operate in low-income, rural areas become more easily profitable and scalable because of technology. Consider the fact that mobile money existed in East Africa at least fifteen years before Venmo took off in America, and you can see how much potential exists in these areas. Africa still maintains the highest penetration of mobile money on the planet, and elsewhere, nine hundred million Indians are ready to go cashless. Impact investing provides access to untapped markets, which makes being a conscious investor about more than simply doing good. From a business perspective, a conscious approach to investing can create a profitable opportunity.

The purpose-driven business's mission is to produce services and goods in an efficient and accessible format that is financially sustainable while creating positive impact. A new concept is arising that governments can also be viewed as a form of a purpose-driven entity. From this perspective, governments would use the lenses and tools of philosophy, finance, economics, and practical organization to foster a favorable environment for innovation and for ESG considerations in newly formed business. There are countless examples of emerging market countries adopting this approach and setting an example for others. For example, the drone delivery company Zipline's initial pilot in Rwanda to deliver medical supplies to rural areas began years before the company made headway into the American market.

With great potential comes great temptation, of course, and concepts and practices like *impact washing* and *green washing* are important to look out for. Companies might pursue certifications and labels like ESG, but often, they do not live up to their stated values. They do not consider potentially harmful side effects of their approach, or they otherwise are not committed to creating impact in a genuine way. They might also use purported impact as a veil to attract investors, even when social and environmental impact criteria have not been considered at all.

In light of these disingenuous claims, investors and advisors alike are asking more questions and demanding more authentic impact investing offerings with better accountability. Meanwhile, the philanthropy sector has realized that the key for success is engaging with private markets.

Philanthropy is still crucial. In fact, there are some areas in which impact investing is *not* the most effective approach. There is definitely a place in society for philanthropy—sometimes, it is the perfect tool, like with disaster relief. Programs that do not have consistent funding struggle to be sustainable. But many donations are one-time transactions. How can an organization grow and innovate if it constantly has funding shortages? However, in general, we as a culture have become more interested in conscious investing because of its increased sustainability, as well as its growth and scaling potential.

Think of conscious investing as a sustainable alternative to traditional investing that has greater potential for scaling impact than philanthropy—one that comes with a triple-bottom-line return: you can make money, you can have a social impact, and you can have an environmental impact, all in one investment. In that way, conscious investment goes beyond the transactional nature of our current system of capitalism.

In these exceptional times, many of our challenges can be solved with the capital and technology already available on the planet. When we pair our ingenuity and resources with emotional awareness and concern for one another, we can achieve greatness.

JEFFREY'S STORY

Jeffrey Brown operates thirteen supermarkets in the Philadelphia area. Brown's Super Stores are mostly located in underserved communities—food deserts and places where residents lack access to healthy options. Jeffrey has taken a holistic approach to being community-oriented in his supermarket model.

Here is what that means in practical terms. According to the USDA, 36.5 million Americans live in low-income areas with limited access to supermarkets. Seventeen million have to travel over twenty miles to get to the nearest store. As you can imagine, a lack of access to healthy foods has an enormous effect on health and insurance costs. All told, the direct and indirect health-related costs of food insecurity in the United States are over $160 billion.

When he started Brown's Super Stores, Jeffrey's initial mission was to eliminate these food deserts and provide good quality food to underserved communities. As the company grew, he saw an exciting opportunity to continue serving his market. He also increased the revenue significantly when he took over existing supermarkets in food deserts.

In very practical and inspiring ways, Jeffrey's company is innovating ways to build a business model and be inclusive of his community's specific needs. Since its creation, Brown's Super Stores has created three thousand jobs—including seven hundred individuals who were formerly incarcerated, making it one of the largest ex-convict hiring programs in the country. Each supermarket has a health clinic and a credit union, where customers can open bank accounts that are capable of having a zero balance, and they regularly host community meetings to solicit feedback.

Notice how one big mission can open the doors to so many smaller sources of impact? Your current life, routine, business, work, and investments can serve a greater purpose, as long as you keep that purpose top of mind along the way.[54]

BUILDING BEYOND CAPITAL

In 2009, I was set on using my skills and resources to create a positive impact. While philanthropy seemed like an obvious choice, I envisioned an approach to contributing beyond myself that was better aligned with my vision: to use my skills, live by my values, and honor my upbringing.

The first part of that vision centered on sustainability. Philanthropy plays an important role in our society, but its reach and potential for impact are limited. If we could create sustainable businesses through the investment of our time, money, and network—while inculcating sustainability into companies by seeking a return—my skills and investments could be used toward greater potential than traditional donations would have offered.

The second part of that vision acknowledged the expectation that foundations operate on a lean budget, often restricting their potential impact. Contrasting those limitations against the potential market opportunity outlined in *The Next 4 Billion*, my husband, Hooman, and I developed a thesis around impact investing rather than direct philanthropy. We set up as a nonprofit to help create a landscape where young, socially oriented businesses could thrive. That way, it would be easier for us to pave the way for other investors to invest with a purely for-profit mindset later on.

At the core of this thesis was the question about where our money, time, and skills would be most effective. Without having the resources of philanthropists like Bill and Melinda Gates, we could not invest large sums of money all at once. Instead, we took an approach that aligned more closely with Singer's *child in the pond* example. We were confident that a small amount of greatly needed capital could go a long way if invested systematically and in a highly considered fashion.

We saw an opportunity to invest in purpose-driven businesses providing access to basic goods and services to low-income populations. As a solution, we made seed investments in countries whose populations fit this description and possessed other market dynamics that could support startup investments: financial growth, mobile prevalence, lean startup capabilities, and ubiquity of technology. We also aimed to invest in the visionaries behind the enterprise, many of whom were implementing The CEO Mindset and serving as conscious leaders for all the stakeholders they were serving. With our starting point established, we founded Beyond Capital and set out to make our first investment.

At the same time, we also began recruiting our network to join our work in order to raise awareness, gather resources, and build support, so we could spark a larger conversation about what business as a force for good could be. We met many working professionals who wanted to give back. Some of these professionals were fresh out of business school, some became board members, and some were pro-bono collaborators from institutions such as law firms and financial modeling assistance firms. They did not have the capital to contribute financially, but they *did* have time and skill. With the support of these high-caliber professionals, we have continued to invest as a venture capital fund with a social mission. As of this writing, Beyond Capital and our portfolio companies have received nearly $2.5 million worth of pro-bono contributions of time and resource.

I am proud of what we have already accomplished, though I am confident that we have a productive future ahead. We exited one investment, ERC Eyecare, and doubled our money while improving access to glasses and cataract surgery for one hundred fifty thousand people. Since then, as of this writing the company has provided eye care access to over three hundred thousand people. On the heels of the success of a company like ERC Eyecare, we reinvest that multiplied capital into more promising purpose-driven companies. Driven by this sustainable approach, we anticipate a future that includes dozens more investments into purpose-driven businesses.

Even though we plan to close our for-profit venture fund in 2021, we consistently see the positive benefits of having roots as a nonprofit venture fund because we have proven that our fidelity is to the social impact of our work, and our goal is genuine: to inspire sustainability and profitability into the companies we fund.

At our core, we are a venture fund. When we started investing this way, venture investing in our target markets was not viewed as trendy or cool; it was viewed as risky and unproven. We had to prove through our work, staying power, and track record that impact investing is not only a viable way to invest your money but it is also *the* way forward for those seeking to do good and make money at the same time.

Building on top of this core, we have added a more communicative strategy, which includes efforts like *The Conscious Investor* online magazine, *The Beyond Capital Podcast*, and the events and gatherings we hold for the members of our Ambassador Program. From there, our goal has been to scale our message to inspire others to think differently (and this book has been part of that effort). Over the years, our brand has mattered inside and outside of the countries where we have invested, with entrepreneurs, donors, and investors. In our unique way, then, we continue to speak to a wider audience about impact investing in order to grow and scale awareness of our work and the industry at large.

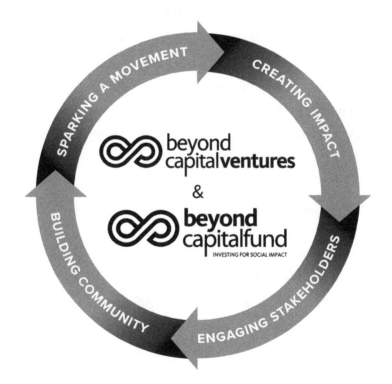

find your cause

Between 1990 and 2020, childhood obesity has tripled.[55] By July 2020, according to some estimates, 13.9 million children lived in homes that were food insecure.[56] One possible solution, according to a UC

Berkeley study, is to provide healthy school meals for children, which has a positive correlation to academic outcomes.[57] This became the driving cause for a purpose-driven company called Revolution Foods.

Started in 2005, Revolution Foods is a registered B Corporation that serves 2.5 million meals a week—including 1.2 million servings of fruit—to American schoolchildren in four hundred cities around the country. Uniquely, Revolution Foods involves kids in the meal-creation process, from asking them what they want to eat to hosting cooking classes that teach them how to make their favorite recipes at home. In this way, they directly address food insecurity for low-income students, ranked as one of the healthiest school meal providers in the United States.

The CEO of Revolution Foods, Kristin Richmond, comes from a background in finance and social entrepreneurship, and her goal was to not only provide healthy school lunches but also to change the way children in America approach food. By centering the business around good quality food, Revolution Foods could also work to reduce obesity, promote a healthy lifestyle, and reduce food waste. Revolution Foods collaborates with schools to provide the right portion sizes for children and uses locally sourced produce to minimize environmental harm and create a sustainable supply chain. The result is a company that does not have a negative impact on the environment to source food and can grow at scale.

Though Revolution Foods is a profitable company, it is also one with a social and environmental mission actively aiming to be a force for good. As their example shows, intentionality and purpose can be the main drivers of success, creating opportunity for both investor and beneficiary alike. The only thing left is to find the cause that will spark your interest, joy, and passion.

When many of us think about doing good, we often think in abstracts. Try simplifying your mission to evaluate what you really want to achieve. Even if the next steps are complicated, defining your purpose will provide a sense of clarity for the rest of your mission.

Everybody has something they care deeply about, often guided by life experience. Some are passionate about the climate crisis, while others are interested in tackling childhood wellness. At Beyond Capital, our mission is to invest in companies that provide access to basic goods and services, improving the standard of living for those living on less than fifteen dollars a day and often at the bottom of the global economic pyramid.

We are lucky enough to live in a time where we can have a material impact on a social problem with little sacrifice in our own lives. This makes it our moral imperative to do good, and a conscious use of impact investing makes that imperative practical and obtainable.

is doing good good enough?

In the next chapter, I will begin to show you how to apply this framework for doing good in the context of impact investing. But first, I want to address the elephant in the room: is doing good actually good enough?

Doing good lies at the core of conscious investing. However, doing good *successfully* means considering the impact your actions will have and what unintended consequences they might have.

The tragic experience of one friend working in the medical device industry illustrates what I mean. As part of his work, this executive traveled to Chiapas, Mexico to see what the company's social responsibility efforts were contributing to. During this visit, he was able to assist with a child who was having his cleft palate repair surgery. He found the experience so moving that he asked if he could take a picture with the boy for the company newsletter.

A year later, the executive checked back in, asking the doctor who returned for another round of surgeries if he could follow up with the child, take another picture, and share an update on the story for the company newsletter. The doctor explained that was impossible. Sadly, the child had passed away from septic shock not long after his surgery. Because the boy lived in a remote area, once he fell ill, he could not be treated.

This story is an important reminder that, sometimes, doing good can have other consequences. This executive and his medical device company had good intentions, but those intentions were not sustainable—and they brought with them unintended consequences. If you think of impact, often the result in isolation is not what you hoped it would be. In fact, it can even be detrimental. This company put a lot of time and effort into arranging the cleft palate surgeries, but ultimately, the effort cost the boy his life.

Your actions do not exist in a vacuum. If you are not aware of this, then even the most well-intentioned efforts risk doing more harm than good from time to time. A critical component of creating a positive impact is understanding the environment in which you are acting.

This perspective lies at the core of a concept known as *systems change*. Systems change is focused on first identifying the root causes of social and environmental problems and then addressing them in practical and holistic ways. Such an approach requires a certain degree of intersectionality. For instance, an issue that at first appears rooted in climate change may also involve issues of poverty and gender. Recognizing the system in which an area of focus exists provides a greater lens and awareness of the components and structures that cause the system to behave in a certain way.

In general, there is a benefit for conscious investors who remain aware that their investments fit into a larger system since it means they are not creating another problem with a solution. At Beyond Capital, before we invest in a company, we are careful to look not only at their intentions but also at their business model to determine whether their efforts are: (1) sustainable, and (2) do not inadvertently extract more value than they provide. While ESG factors can be a useful metric, ESG metric systems often do not measure deeply enough. We are interested not only in the surface-level indicators highlighted by ESG frameworks but also the deeper aspects of the impact companies can have.

For example, East Africa Fruit Farms is a production, trading, and distribution business aimed at minimizing post-harvest losses in Tanzania by buying directly from smallholder farmers—increasing their average income—and delivering to major purchasers and local markets via cold chain logistics. As a business, East Africa Fruit Farms controls the whole value chain, from farming to grading and storing produce and to selling to hotels, restaurants, and supermarkets. Rather than giving farmers agricultural inputs and telling them what to grow, the company helps farmers generate knowledge on how to produce greater crop yield. East Africa Fruit Farms then will determine where to sell their produce and how to otherwise maximize their value chain.

In doing so, East Africa Fruit Farms has helped to increase the annual income of the farmers the company works with to over $1,600 a year—a threefold increase for a community whose average earnings are a dollar a day. As of this writing, East Africa Fruit Farms has improved the livelihoods of 1,943 smallholder farmers.

As much as it is important to question what you own, it is also important to question the broader impact your investments are having and will have when you align your money with your values. This question is key to the process of the impact measurement of your investments, which begins by asking deeper questions based on the following two factors:

- What is the impact of my investment, from a systems-change perspective?
- How sustainable is the company or effort I am supporting to bring forth change for the long term?

Regarding sustainability, if you are investing in a company already listed on the stock exchange, then it is assumed that company has readily available access to capital. While this refers to financial sustainability, here we are addressing sustainability from the perspective of the social and environmental mission of that company. Will this business live up to its promise of putting women on its board of directors, for example—not just in a superficial manner but in a way that gives women meaningful roles, ensures their voices are considered, and fosters long-term change to the position of women in leadership?

The more questions asked, the more you will know, the more methodological you can be in practicing conscious investing, and the more successful those efforts are likely to be. Seasoned investors are already intentional about where they invest. In that way, conscious investing is no different; you are just focusing on factors other than profitability or returns alone.

In the simplest possible terms, the best approach is to ask questions. If an advisor, investment manager, or company founder has not done the necessary due diligence or is otherwise unable to provide a clear answer to your questions, then that is an indicator that this may not be the best opportunity for you to create the impact you are looking for.

If you are concerned about potential negative consequences of your conscious investing, try to be as diligent as possible, but know that you are making progress by putting your resources behind an investment that meets your goals. I still believe that doing some good is a step in the right direction. For example, a vegetarian does not save *all* the animals, but over their lifetime, they *will* have saved about seven thousand of them.

Remember, your voice, your actions, and your consumer choices also comprise your impact, and those are tools that can complement your investments.

CHAPTER 4

pursuing good through conscious investing

My quantitative mind and fondness for spreadsheets drew me to finance from an early age. Later on, as I developed my career on Wall Street, books like *Rich Dad, Poor Dad* helped me reframe my thinking, especially for when I became a parent. If we are not the ones to talk to our kids about seemingly difficult topics, then who will? The more my consciousness grew, the more I wanted to share with my kids. I quickly learned that this kind of openness often creates a two-way dialogue. We learn as much from them as they do from us.

At the age of four, my son, Alessandro, learned about "Trash Island" in school and was so affected by it that he came home with concerns and questions. Trash Island is also known as the Great Pacific Garbage Patch or the Plastic Trash Vortex. It is a large collection of relatively small pieces of plastic and other trash in the Pacific Ocean, covering almost one million square miles. Animals can become trapped in plastic nets and rings, and some long-lasting plastics also end up in the stomachs of marine animals, which can lead to greater problems throughout the food chain. The problem is so severe that the United Nations Ocean Conference estimated that the oceans might contain more weight in plastics than fish by the year 2050.[58]

My son takes these conversations seriously. He would hate to think that something he did contributed to making Trash Island even worse than it already was! However, he does not always understand what actually creates trash or where it comes from. It is up to me to connect those broader lessons to everyday reality. If we are at a restaurant and he starts playing with plastic straws, or when he uses polystyrene cups lying around at his tennis lesson, I gently mention that these items may one day end up in Trash Island.

Inspired by our conversations, I decided to tie in my conscious investing with Alessandro's passion for positive change. I began investing a small amount of money with him each month—$100 at first, and later $250—into the Aspiration Redwood Fund. This fund, which is accessible to anybody, invests in public companies that are screened for ESG criteria. According to Aspiration, also a B Corporation bank, "Smart companies know that if they act better, they will do better." To live up to that value, the Aspiration Redwood

Fund focuses on fossil-fuel-free fund investing, as well as on businesses that care about their people, the planet, and creating a green purpose and mission.

By making small, regular contributions, I am able to feel good about money that I hardly notice now, but that I know will add up over time. A $250 monthly investment compounding over twenty years should easily be worth $80,000—and likely $100,000 or more. One day, that investment capital will become Alessandro's and his sister's. When that day comes, hopefully he will feel empowered to make his own informed choices and become a conscious investor himself.

If I were to hand him that sum as a young adult, that kind of gift could be detrimental to his own wealth consciousness. As part of a family with all our needs met, I am mindful of raising a child who, on one hand, does not exhibit the traits of *affluenza* (that is, he is not spoiled) but who, on the other hand, knows his place as a global citizen, understands wealth consciousness, and has a mindset of abundance. However, by talking to him about the financial return of his money, as well as the good it can accomplish, the investment becomes a tool to teach him about awareness, service, and passion in a meaningful and tangible way—in other words, money has value beyond solely financial return.

Of course, much of that payoff will not come until he is older. For now, I simply explain to him in broad terms how I invest and spend my resources and why. Slowly, the idea that money can have an impact on the issues he cares about will begin to take shape in his mind and provide him with a solid foundation for using money to do good later in his life. For now, he wants to grow up to be an inventor working with ocean plastic.

Our values are shaped in childhood and often stick with us long into adulthood. Just as I am helping Alessandro connect to his own environmental concerns, I have invested in efforts that I watched my family support while I was growing up. My grandmother and grandfather, a medical doctor, moved their family from the United States to rural Tanzania in order to establish a hospital, and today, I am incredibly proud to have over 30 percent of the portfolio at Beyond Capital invested in healthcare education, digital healthcare, at-home care, and healthcare mobility. Conscious investing connects our time, money, and networks with the people and causes that we care about.

In our family, we believe in boundless possibilities. It is a mindset that has inspired entrepreneurship, resilience, lifelong relationships, and fun in our lives. In teaching this mindset to the next generation of our family, we aim to inspire consciousness in all areas. As if our family was a company, we think of all stakeholders in most all decisions we make. Not only is it important to teach our children this level of awareness but to also set up a mindset of possibility that conscious investing is possible, can be rewarding, and can allow for our children to find meaning and purpose in their lives.

In practical terms, this could be teaching the next generation to ask deeper questions about where their money is invested and why or discussing why it is important to recycle and significantly reduce the use of single-use plastics in conjunction with ocean health and innovative solutions to upcycling ocean plastic. The possibilities are boundless, and they exist all around us.

How we express these themes can also be holistic, including investing, educating, advocating for, and purchasing in favor of the theme of diminishing Trash Island. And in the end, we get to approach money as a topic in our household that has a far broader reach than just financial return.

informed decisions are better decisions

For my whole adult life, I have always been aware of that person at the dinner party who is falling over himself to tell you about a cannot-miss investment that you would be foolish not to get in on. Often, the investment he is promoting is some sort of tech-driven, direct-to-consumer business that will "revolutionize the way we all buy."

No doubt, many of you reading this have also encountered this type of entrepreneur. I admit my life has been made easier by many direct-to-consumer companies. Even when you are considering investing in this company, the challenge is often that you do not have much in the way of concrete information with which to evaluate the opportunity. There might be some financial projections and market sizing in a slide deck to show you, but they are just projections and past trends—so far, the company is just a startup that has not made any real revenue or profit. Sure, the idea of being an angel investor is appealing, but even more appealing is the idea of being an angel investor with a high probability of seeing a return on your investment.

Impact investing really does offer additional information to evaluate a company from other angles. A purpose-driven company must answer other questions aside from just financial projections. The company must spotlight the beneficiaries of their product or service and share any additional impact it is creating.

For instance, if I were being asked to invest in a purpose-driven houseplant startup, I would need several questions answered before I decided to move forward. To provide a sample:

- What do houseplants do for the people who buy them? Does it give them a better sense of well-being in their homes? Do they contribute to better mental health and purify the air?
- What are the conditions for the people the company hires? Are they marginally employed?
- What is the environmental impact of the supply chain to grow and distribute the plants?

Through questions like these, an impact investor has much more information to determine whether the investment meets their criteria.

To illustrate what this process might look like and how you might get started, I will use my experience with Peloton, a publicly traded fitness company that, at least in regard to initial impressions, has repeatedly surprised me as a user with its multifaceted focus on social impact. As a member, you not only have the opportunity to improve your physical health through the company's fitness programs, but you also feel a sense of community and belonging, no matter your fitness level, body type, skin color, or sexual orientation. From time to time, when I am riding the Peloton stationary bike, I cannot help but wear my investor hat, thinking through how Peloton's brand identity not only allows for users to feel healthy and included but also how employees are encouraged to be their authentic selves and cultivate a community that values diversity and inclusion. Ideally, the company's board could pursue more equal representation of women and people of color. Further, while I have not deeply analyzed the environmental impact of Peloton, working out at home saves energy by eliminating the need to commute to a gym or fitness studio. This, all coupled with a business growing at a rapid pace, would make Peloton a compelling purpose-driven company that is, at the very least, worthy of a deep due-diligence dive.

Not only does a purpose-driven company, by its nature, provide more information to the investor, but it is also a safer bet. Between 2005 and 2015, 90 percent of companies in the S&P 500 that went bankrupt had a low ESG rating.[59] Granted, this may be a small sample size and may be linked to cyclical fluctuations. However, all available evidence points to the fact that purpose-driven companies show double the top-line growth that non-purpose-driven companies produce.

ROSALIE'S IMPACT

Rosalie is from Kigali, Rwanda, the mother to a lovely son and employee of a women's health company based in East Africa, specifically Rwanda and Kenya. The company, Kasha, is an e-commerce platform that provides access to feminine sanitation products, contraceptives, lotions, and other hygiene products for women.

Rosalie earns a sustainable living by selling women's health products locally to the women in her community. The orders are placed digitally, and products are delivered to women in a culturally sensitive way, curbing the social stigma of women's health in Rwanda, Kenya, and many other parts of East Africa and elsewhere.

By providing access to feminine hygiene products and family planning, Rosalie is helping to empower the women in her local community, keeping girls in school. She is able to earn a sustainable income while still creating a massive impact on her corner of the globe.

She is a curious woman who sees the world beyond her village. And when I met her in person in 2018, she even went so far as to ask what products I was using for the women in her village, which spoke to her insightful and entrepreneurial nature.

Kasha is a prime example of a purpose-driven company. It is run by Joanna Bischel, a conscious leader herself who considers all stakeholders in her leadership decisions. Not only does she serve her customers, employees, and shareholders, but Joanna has also worked with the government as a key stakeholder to increase access to contraceptives and pave the way for women's health products to be more widely accessible in the markets where she and her company operate.

shifting our relationship to money

Even well into the twenty-first century, there remains a persistent stigma that keeps us from talking openly about our finances to our family, friends, classmates, and colleagues. There is also a historical tendency for money to be a man's business (this is still common thinking in many parts of the world), leaving women and children out of the conversation. This phenomenon persists in spite of the increasing parity between the wealth of men and women, with women controlling 51 percent of the wealth in the United States and representing an increasingly greater share in the coming decade.[60] Still, a UBS study found that the millennial women it surveyed exhibited less financial independence than the women it surveyed in the baby boomer generation.[61]

This trend has a direct correlation to how women of all generations approach investing. Scholars have long since noticed that the mindset around investing differs between men and women and that the classic narrative around investing is considered masculine.[62] For decades, *outperforming* the market has been the principal sign of male success. Such a pursuit stems from a competitive and/or output-driven mindset. However, while it remains the dominant mindset, this paradigm is shifting. Increasingly, investors are moving toward other factors to evaluate a successful investment strategy that does not just focus on outsized performance, and women specifically have begun to value financial independence more.

Sallie Krawcheck, Co-founder and Chief Executive of Ellevest, has been a leading voice in this conversation. According to Krawcheck,

Ellevest was built around the idea of serving women and encouraging them to engage in conversations and activities surrounding money. For women, money, finance, and investments can be seen as taboo subjects. Finance is a male-dominated field, and women are actively discouraged from participating.

Through Ellevest, Krawcheck is working to break the taboo surrounding women and money—and she is not the only one. Many investing clubs have focused on the tremendous disconnect between women's priorities and what the financial services industry has traditionally emphasized for them. By creating a space for women to join the conversation, women are in turn able to feel more empowered about their financial futures.[63]

This broad conversation has impacted my own work in this field as well. I am often asked about being a female in finance. Traditionally, my stance has been similar to Krawcheck's. I have experienced firsthand the way women are made to feel shame for having investment portfolios and owning assets, but through my position as an impact investor, I have the opportunity to help reframe the conversation: the more we talk about the emotional connection to finances and the meaning behind our money, the more interest there will be in financial literacy.[64]

In 2019, the Organisation for Economic Co-Operation and Development estimated that economic gender inequality costs women in developing nations $9 trillion per year—a sum that would not only give new spending power to women and benefit their families and communities but could also provide a massive boost to the global economy as a whole. The trend is continuing. A recent survey at a private bank showed that 90 percent of women surveyed indicated that they want to invest at least a portion of their wealth in a manner that aligns with their values.[65]

Equally important is the need to understand and address the intersectionality between this issue and other sociopolitical and epidemiological forces. For instance, the COVID-19 pandemic has shown that what happens in one part of the globe can impact people elsewhere and that wealth cannot entirely equalize, neutralize, or even erase the effects of a pandemic in our lives. Perhaps more importantly, it has exposed already existing inequalities in our global system, such as the lack of access to quality healthcare for communities of color and issues of bias surrounding race and medical treatment.[66]

Because it is more socially acceptable to talk about the causes you care about, conscious investing allows you to speak more openly about what you have invested in and gradually shift this paradigm.

A helpful way to reframe your use of money might be to think of it as detoxification. In modern society, you can detox anything. You can detox your cleaning supplies of toxic chemicals. You can buy organic food and nontoxic beauty products. You can pay attention to which toxins and chemicals are around your children and eliminate many of them from your life. Thanks to Marie Kondo, you can even detox negative connections to the very objects in your life by learning to declutter the spaces you commonly occupy.

I have done my share of "detoxing" over the past twenty years, removing chemicals, pesticides, negative thoughts, and toxic relationships from my life. One of my *aha* moments was when I asked myself whether I could detoxify my money of values inconsistent with my own. Like many others, for years, I had not considered this practice simply because I had not realized such an alternative was available. In other aspects of my life (such as my food choices, for instance), I clearly saw the choice between purchasing foods produced with pesticides and chemicals and food produced organically (even if purchasing the latter might come with a markup). Similarly, I knew that the way I spent and invested my money often worked against my own values, though at the time I mistakenly believed I did not have a choice.

Like me, you may have held similar beliefs. While there has been much discussion about how to detox your food choices, there has been far less discussion about how to do the same with your money. Traditional approaches to investing lack transparency and metrics systems for measuring more than the financial return of your investments. Further, even the thought of detoxing your investments often leads to other concerns—specifically, that you might have to sacrifice in other areas (such as returns, wealth, or time) in order to achieve your detoxification goals. This is not the case. Not only can you protect your return through impact investments, but when your investments align your values with your money, it often creates a sense of fulfillment rather than one of loss.

Often, however, this resistance to detoxing can stem an inability to think of money as an emotional force. However, as I have learned over a decade-plus as a conscious investor, it is possible for an investment to spark joy—and not only from a returns perspective. Even the smallest amounts can go toward a significant amount of good. Think about how many small investments can add up to fight climate change, sustainably develop underserved populations, and eradicate neglected tropical diseases like malaria.

Fortunately, through my decision to become a conscious investor and witness firsthand the good my money could do, I learned to retrain these old thoughts and patterns around money. When you fully comprehend the impact that money, investing, and consumer choices can have, you become empowered as an investor in a way that few other passion projects or initiatives can enable. For many investors, knowing there is more than return creates tremendous power to take action, set measurable goals, and exceed financial expectations.

We declutter and detox our lives to create better health and a sense of ease in our lives—the same is true of our money. Impact investing opens the door for more meaningful conversations about money among the gender divide, the generational gap, and disparate socioeconomic brackets.

Nobody wants to be in a difficult financial situation. We are all looking to advance ourselves and our families and live a comfortable life. Both men and women of all socioeconomic backgrounds should feel empowered to ask more from their investments and put their money toward work that makes a difference. Investing in positive impact is good for your well-being, makes you feel good, and is one of the highest energy producers out there.[67]

Conscious investing factors in social and environmental returns, which tap into a core human desire: to belong to a larger community and to participate in society. Think of this as not just asking more of your money but also asking *more of yourself.* The feeling generated from conscious investing will have an impact on all other areas of your life.

CULTIVATING EMOTIONAL CONNECTION TO YOUR MONEY

Right now, think about something you know and love. Perhaps your children or your partner come to mind. You might even think of your home or some nice jewelry. Whatever it is, hold that thought for a moment, and identify the emotions that come with the thought.

Now, try to apply that same sense of emotional connection to your money.

What does it feel like to direct your emotions in this way? Do your current investments inspire joy? If not, you have an opportunity to reallocate that money to a place where it *will.* You actually can create that same emotional connection toward money that you have toward your spouse, your favorite ring, or your cat.

Now, take a moment to think about why money is important. For me, it brings ease, freedom, and support for my family and my career. It might bring a beautiful home for you and your loved ones, an incredible vacation, or even the ability to work on a project that you love. Tapping into the good feelings that money can bring is a first step to aligning your money with your values, which brings peace, harmony, and a clarity of purpose.

There are people I meet who are not interested in conscious investing and feel happy just making money. That is fine. However, to live this way, there are areas, actions, thoughts and behaviors that you are choosing to ignore. At some point, they may find that money will not be enough. Now more than ever, it is the time to become conscious—to consider your investments and spending a source of wellness, power, and joy. As we connect emotionally to our money and investments, there may be some cognitive biases along the way that need to be worked through.

HOW MUCH CAN MONEY REALLY BUY?

Keren Eldad is a good friend as well as my executive coach. With an extensive network of over 1,200 clients, she has learned a great deal about our behaviors, our alignment, and what brings us success and joy. And she has observed an inverse correlation between financial success and happiness.

If you feel unhappy because of your financial success or feel overwhelmed because you have too many choices in life, you are not alone. And you do not have to stay that way. In other words, there are other types of wealth than just money. Both Coach Keren and I enjoy a good vacation and a nice pair of shoes. We share a love for the peace of mind that comes with being in a beautiful place, eating great food, and relaxing by the beach. However, I have learned to look for more to feed my soul. Wealth by itself is boring. There is a limited amount of truly fulfilling goods, services, and experiences that money can buy. Impact investing allows you to do more with your money by helping you to feed your soul, find peace, and create harmony.

HOW MUCH RETURN IS ENOUGH?

Investors inevitably have to ask themselves what an appropriate return is on their investment. Depending on whom you ask, that is going to be a different number. For some investors, doubling their money is not enough. For others, it is plenty.

From a conscious investing perspective, the more investors expect these kinds of outsized returns, the more they risk crossing that line from being impactful to being extractive.

Granted, there is a lot of gray area on either side of this line. But this ambiguity is precisely why it is so important to define that line for yourself. To help define it, ask: Is your investment extracting value or adding value? Would you be happy to know you are benefitting potentially at the exclusion of others?

During the COVID-19 pandemic, I was fortunate that my basic needs were still met. Instead of struggling to survive in the present, this allowed me to think about my future. What do I need to live, not just until I am sixty but until I am one hundred or older? From that frame of mind, what is excess, and what is truly enough?

impact in action

In 2017, I had the opportunity to travel to India to meet with the team at Karma Healthcare, which provides telemedicine solutions in rural areas of the country. We stopped at the home of a four-year-old girl and spoke to her parents about the lack of accessibility to healthcare in their region. Her parents live under the government-defined poverty line and were given a card by the Indian government to prove that status for the purpose of access to certain goods and services. As an investor, my purpose for visiting their home was to verify how access to healthcare would impact the life of somebody at this level of income.

When we directed them to Karma Healthcare, they were willing to spend the small budget that they had for healthcare at the Karma Healthcare clinic down the road. They were pleased that they could actually treat their daughter at an affordable price.

When I was at the clinic in India, I saw four patients walk through the door in a thirty-minute period. For a very rural area with a relatively low population, this was a heartening picture of how well the clinic was reaching its community.

One gentleman who came in looked very sick, like he had the flu. He waited for the nurse to take his vital signs, which she would send to the doctor so the doctor could come on screen and chat with the patient. When the man's name was called, I have never seen anyone stand up with as much intention as he did, despite being so ill. This was a repeat patient who felt good about the care he was going to receive. While healthcare access is a personal passion of mine, seeing our investments in action, improving real people's lives, was a remarkable experience.

BRIAN'S SECOND CAREER

When we started Beyond Capital, my husband, Hooman, and I knew we could not run a venture fund on our own. Luckily, we were buoyed by a wave of young professionals who were interested in the impact investing space and willing to get involved. For instance, Brian Axelrad, our very first applicant and intern, ended up becoming our Chief Investment Officer. Eight years ago, he signed on to twenty-five hours of investment work a month, to help Beyond Capital find and invest in the most legitimate and viable companies with a promise of social impact. Among the team, he is famous for having told us, "I am having my second career at the same time as my first."

Brian's volunteer mission is all the more special because it is a win-win. I have met a lot of lawyers, and I can confidently say Brian is the smartest lawyer I have ever observed. He attended the University of Michigan and has two graduate degrees—an MBA from the University of Chicago and a legal degree from Northwestern University. Volunteering his time is a way for Brian to use his skills for good while finding incredible personal fulfillment. In doing so, he became a conscious investor.

going all in

Beyond Capital and I were among the original members of Toniic, a global community of asset owners seeking deeper positive net impact across the spectrum of capital. One of the ways Toniic achieves this is through the 100% Impact Network, which focuses on a range of investment approaches, from individual investors to fund managers, who are all equally committed to creating impact with their investment decisions. For some, the goal is for their portfolio to be completely aligned and consistent with their values. Toniic refers to this as "going all in."

For Beyond Capital and the growing community of impact investors, conscious investing is not just about one company in rural India. It is about sparking a movement. There are over 400 Toniic members, and we are all deeply committed to creating impact with our money. The impact metrics, such as number of individual lives impacted through investments, if we were to calculate it, would be immense.

Nearly all of us have been raised to discern two key areas in life: the first is the values in our day-to-day lives, and the second is our money—how we make it, how we spend it, and the quality of life it affords. Impact investing brings these two paths together. For me, this has created a new sense of fulfillment and allowed me to pursue my genuine passion while still creating a measurable impact for the causes I care about. Aligning your values with your money creates a beautiful sense of unity not only within yourself but also within a larger network of like-minded individuals. Further, it has also strengthened my sense of belonging to a global community. Above all, I feel most connected to the people my investments serve, like Rosalie. When I first met her in person in Rwanda in 2018, I was nervous, like meeting a long-lost family member. As we spoke, I realized we had common interests and that we each had a son. We may have had different upbringings, but we were both mothers and working women. We often have more to relate to others than we might think, and conscious investing can help find this common ground.

Growing up with a family living in Africa and as a middle-class girl of Eastern European heritage in New York City, my privilege was ever present. As an investor in markets with structural inequalities and deeply biased financial systems, I observe many who take advantage of such power dynamics. But they often miss what is more for investors that are integrating positive impact into their investments. It is community and connection. While I may never know why I am separated from Rosalie in so many ways, I do know we are both human, and investing in companies like Kasha has made me feel more connected to women like her than ever.

Ultimately, the most inspiring thing about conscious investing—for me and for most others I speak to—is simply knowing that conscious investing is possible. As soon as I realized I could bring greater consciousness to my investments and consumer choices, and that doing so would bring tremendous value to my life, I was filled with an immense amount of energy, unity, and power.

Now that you have realized the possibilities as well, is anything stopping you from going all in?

the next step

So far, we have looked inward into ourselves and understood the framework for doing good and how principles of leadership and other resources play a role. Through my experience building Beyond Capital—and through getting to know businesses like Revolution Foods, Karma, and others—I have personally felt the potential becoming a conscious investor can have.

Conscious investing is your opportunity to seize. Your time, consumerist habits, money, investments, and the mark you leave are all part of the value that you can create. You can choose what that value will reflect and what your legacy will look like.

Think about the last time you wanted to buy a specific car for yourself. Suddenly, you saw that car everywhere. The exact same thing can happen with your values. Once you define your passion or area of concern, more areas of your life will open up space to have an impact. Before you know it, you will find yourself with more opportunities than ever before.

As you move into part two of this book, remember that you do not have to sell everything and change your life all at once. This is a process, a transition in which you have an opportunity to offer yourself kindness. Identify the areas of your life that are currently in direct conflict with your values, but be realistic about the way your values can be lived. Trust the experience, allow yourself to be empowered, and know that you are not alone. The next step is just to get started.

part 2

what can you do today?

I believe success is always defined by a process, and a systematic approach to achieving your goal yields the strongest results. This is why, in Part 2, you will be guided toward becoming a conscious investor with clear, sequential steps. Here, I will answer some of the most common questions about impact investing—such as "Where do I start?" and "What questions do I ask?" As you will discover, the first step is to define your values and the issues you care about (knowing that this can be an ongoing exercise).

As Maya Angelou said, "Do the best you can until you know better. When you know better, do better." Do not wait for perfection. Rather, understand the value of leading with your values. A good starting point can be to truly discover what you own. Use a gut check: Do you feel good about what investments you hold, or where your bank is lending your money on your behalf? Do you feel good about the companies you are currently supporting with your consumer choices? This foundational work will lead to greater ease in investing with awareness and confidence in knowing that the strategy of financial return and positive impact can work for you. Alongside aligning your portfolio, you will also understand the importance of developing a community and using other resources to fully live your values.

BECOMING A CONSCIOUS INVESTOR

1. Define your values. What are you passionate about?
2. Recognize the importance of living your life by leading with your values.
3. Practice being wealth conscious. Set your idea of wealth to one of abundance.
4. Know what you own and review your options carefully to ensure your resources are being invested in line with your values.
5. Appreciate the fact that you can generate social and financial return.
6. Surround yourself with a community that supports your impact goals.
7. Be a discerning consumer and an active citizen.

CHAPTER 5

define
your values

I n 1959, my paternal grandfather moved my dad and his sib-
lings from the United States to Tanzania to establish a health
clinic. Back in the Midwest of the United States, my maternal
grandfather was also involved in poverty alleviation and economic
development.

Growing up, I was inspired by my maternal grandfather, Edward
Bonior, who was a World War II veteran, stood at six foot, four inches
tall, and was in charge of the Office of Economic Opportunity as part
of the War on Poverty, a legislative agenda created by Lyndon B.

Johnson. In 1997, at his funeral, my family heard from the many individuals who were inspired by his work and his life. Many others told us how he had made an immeasurable difference in their economic or financial situation because he cared and possessed intention in his work. Seeing the examples on both sides of my family set the tone for what I would come to believe in and advocate for as an adult.

In my family, I am thought of as the finance investment expert. Mine is a different path than that of my parents and grandparents, but over the years, I have independently examined each of the values I was raised with and can confirm that they are equally as important to me. They taught me to contribute beyond myself and to make strides for equality and justice. It is why I support job creation for women in India, access to basic healthcare for women in East Africa, and innovative basic-goods-and-services businesses in the Beyond Capital portfolio. And it is why I look for what more my portfolio can do to have an impact—because clearly defined values help me see the steps I need to take to align them with my actions and investments. I am excited by the combination of investing and solving social problems, and that passion keeps me motivated to make change almost every single day. My efficient-minded side also likes the ability to kill two birds with one stone and have my money working directly toward my goals. (I have a mathematics undergraduate degree, which drives a lot of my optimized decision-making.)

On the path to conscious investing, defining your values up front is the most important thing you can do, as it will yield results. It is your decision how you want to create impact. In some cases, you might be the only person focusing on your particular area of interest (although that is unlikely). Think back to the #MeToo movement, for example. That movement started with a single woman, Tarana Burke, standing up and calling out behavior which was unacceptable and inconsistent with her values. Similarly, impact investing started with just a handful of investors who wanted to contribute to valuable causes and find solutions to social problems in ways that extended beyond philanthropy.

Your values are exactly that—yours. They might include caring about gender equality, supporting education, or protecting the environment. They can be varied or specific, and they will likely differ from your neighbor's or your best friend's. Whatever your values are, the process through which you define them is an important one and worth the effort if you wish to begin investing for impact.

discerning your values

The values that drive us to do good are different for everybody. For me, the areas I wish to contribute toward are gender equality, zero poverty, diversity and inclusion, climate action, and education—all in accordance with the Sustainable Development Goals. To begin defining your own values and areas of focus, start by examining your upbringing. It is likely that what you grew up to care about—and what your family raised you to value—will have shaped your own beliefs.

For instance, my uncle, David Bonior, was a historian and lifelong politician, serving in the United States House of Representatives from 1977 to 2003 as both Majority and Minority Whip during his tenure. A dedicated environmentalist, my uncle also sought novel ways to incorporate his values into his campaign strategy. For instance, when out on the campaign trail, he would often either plant trees or even hand out small trees for his constituents to take home and plant. This both helped raise awareness for a cause that was important to him and served to bring the community together. I may not have followed in my uncle's footsteps directly, but I do look for other ways to express my belief in climate action and have learned a great deal from him. Through my own actions, I have found ways to put my own spin on a cause that is meaningful to me. While I do not have a career in politics, I am an active citizen, occasionally raising money for political candidates. Uncle David believes that everybody should be involved in some level of politics—school board races, city council, at both state and federal levels. One of his favorite sayings is, "Democracy is a verb." From his perspective, if we do not all participate, then we forfeit our voice—and, potentially, our democracy. He has encouraged me to think about treating the political system as a positive community engagement tool. While it is said that politics can be "dirty," without active citizens with good social values, we could (and have) inadvertently pursue (pursued) values that are undemocratic.

While family values are a useful way to understand the forces that shape your values, your lived experience is another. For instance, I have been aware of my privilege since childhood. The daughter of two teachers and working artists living in New York City, I grew up in a neighborhood where there were few other white families. It was clear to me that I and my parents were different—not just because of the color of our skin but because of the privileges we were afforded as a result. I had the bigger house, I had the better-quality education, and I had the parents with better access to borrowing who could help fund my Ivy League higher-education tuition.

Seeing what I had access to that many of my neighbors did not—recognizing my privilege—left me with the profound feeling that society should be different. As a result, I formed the core belief that it was my responsibility to seek equality and justice for all. Additionally, I formed the belief that others with privilege have a responsibility to be conscious as well.

Living according to your values should feel easy. When you are connected to the causes and qualities that inspire you to contribute beyond yourself, you have the fuel to wake up and do more every day. The more you contribute to what you believe in, the happier and more fulfilled your life will be. In fact, a feeling of contributing beyond yourself is a feature of success.[68]

Think back to a time when you worked on a project that you felt strongly about. How quickly did time go by? Purpose has a magical quality to it—when you are working on something that is important to you, the hours fly by without you even realizing. That is what living according to your values feels like. It does not feel like an impossible effort. The goals become much more attainable because of the excitement and passion surrounding them.

Defining values does not have to be laborious or difficult. Start with an attitude of openness and eagerness, and simply think about the experiences, beliefs, and relationships that have impacted your life in a big way. Ask yourself what excites you. Think about where you are already giving your money and time.

Pay attention to the days where you feel energized and motivated to get out of bed and get to work. By evaluating these emotions and actions, you can dig deeper into who you are and what you value. When you understand what drives you to do good, you can let those same values drive your investments.

begin now

Impact investing is a real industry with real opportunities, which means it offers many choices. Be as specific and focused as possible when defining your values. Broad themes like gender equality can be expressed in different ways or in different investments—for example, women on boards, women-run businesses, companies serving female consumers better with products and services, businesses employing women, more businesses with good maternity leave policies, and businesses with pay parity between men and women.

Once you start to unpack a term like "gender equality," the options grow exponentially. To account for this, try taking a more thematic approach to impact investing by dedicating a large part of your portfolio—or even your entire portfolio—toward a particular social or environmental theme. This approach is known as *thematic impact investing*. The more specific you are with your values and areas of focus, the easier it will be to make effective choices and apply that theme to your entire portfolio.

For instance, while a theme of gender equality might present an unmanageable number of options, searching for companies with a high percentage of female employees, access to quality daycare centers, or a good family leave policy will produce a much narrower list of opportunities. Plus, focusing on these specific themes ensures total alignment with the broader theme of gender equality.

Once you begin to narrow your values to the details of impact, I find it affects every aspect of your life. I care deeply about the environment and the impact that my carbon footprint will have on future generations. However, for a long time I did not think twice about certain conveniences that were ingrained in my day-to-day existence. After I identified climate action as one of my core values, I began seeing my daily choices in a new light. This is not to say I magically changed overnight. I still use single-use plastics from time to time, even though I know they are inconsistent with my values. But since I cannot unsee the impact of my choices, this is one example of a behavior I am rapidly changing.

In some cases, it is not about swapping out a product or giving up a service. To live out some values, you might decide to spend more volunteer time in a certain place. If homelessness is a cause you are passionate about, for instance, you might visit a food bank to serve the homeless rather than taking a vacation to the beach.

The more you live according to your values, the more they become a lens through which you can view both the world and your investments. Just keep in mind that it does not all have to happen at once and that it is acceptable to have diverse interests. Many impact areas are interrelated, sometimes in surprising ways (climate and women's empowerment, for example). Do not expect to wake up one day to find you have suddenly aligned with your

values in all areas of life. Take your first steps, grow your awareness, learn the language of conscious investing, and let the process
unfold from there.

the values game

Jennifer Kenning, the founder of Align Impact, remembers a time
when no one knew what impact investing meant. Ten years ago, it
was just a niche industry, although most of her clients felt disen-
chanted by treadmill philanthropy. They felt like they were writing
checks without getting any return, with a common desire to do *more*
and no indication of what that might look like.

Kenning also felt motivated to become part of the movement to
change the ineffectiveness of philanthropy. During this time, she
observed multiple trends. For example, she noticed that foundations
were only giving away 5 percent of their endowment. The other 95
percent was invested in an area that was inconsistent with the foundation's supposed mission. Thus, Align Impact was born, where she
now advises clients to have the most legitimate and viable social and
environmental impact with their investments.

By 2020, Kenning accumulated over a decade's worth of academic, institutional, and performance data showing how well
impact investing performs. The problem with impact investing, she
discovered, has not been with the returns but rather with the out-
dated infrastructure of capitalism.

To assist her clients in defining their personal mission and vision
for impact to guide their choices, Kenning uses a specific exercise

that can be considered a values game. She starts by asking them one question: "If you could move the needle in only one thing, what would that be and why?" Then, she assesses her clients' already-existing portfolio to identify where they are currently investing.

If, like many of Kenning's clients, you are a compassionate person, your interests likely span more than just one issue. In such a case, Kenning gives her clients nine high-level categories by which to rank their greatest areas of interest.

Each client gets a hundred chips to distribute across the categories. The values listed include energy and the environment to religious and spiritual causes to impulsive giving. Basic human rights like clean food and water, healthcare, education, and the arts are also included in the areas of focus to choose from. As her clients consider those issues in order of passion or concern, Kenning encourages them to think about more specific areas where they could focus their impact in light of those choices.

This exercise can be challenging, and honestly, that is the point. Kenning's approach is so effective in that it encourages her clients to identify what they *want* to do and then compares that with what they are already supporting or investing in to see if these two areas match.

Through this exercise, not only do clients systematically define their overarching values, but they also come to understand the weighting of certain focus areas over others. Then, based on the results of the game, Kenning gains a better understanding of how to approach that client's portfolio from an impact perspective.

This work is called portfolio allocation, which is the most basic form of understanding where you (or a financial advisor) will invest your money. Much of your portfolio allocation will be driven by investment risk tolerance and the areas you feel passionate about, then allocated by impact goals.

If you do not want to play Kenning's full investment allocation game, I encourage you to at least write down a mission and vision statement for your conscious investing strategy and, specifically, write down your area of focus. Feel free to use the following table to gain inspiration, or simply ask yourself this: how would you contribute beyond yourself if you knew you could not fail?

You will sometimes fail, of course. That is true of any investment. The point is to free yourself to think of the potential and unveil the issues that you would most like to contribute toward. For example, with your time and resources, you could make a dent in criminal justice reform, education, healthcare, gender equality, pandemic response, poverty alleviation, diversity and inclusion, climate action, homelessness, and refugees.

Within each of those areas are several different ways to offer your support. The following table offers some specific examples that should inspire more nuance and depth in your approach. Most often, you can aim to invest in more than one issue within a theme in order to have an impact on the system in which that area exists. Employing a holistic approach in your portfolio is often referred to as a thematic approach. The table below is not exhaustive, rather intended for you to think more holistically about how your values may play a larger role in society and how you can address the whole area of your intended impact.

Area of Impact	Thematic Approach Areas
Environmental conservation	• Clean energy solutions • Climate action • Clean oceans • The intersection of climate change and poverty and/or gender
Scholarship programs	• Investing in charter schools • Early childhood education in marginalized or low-income areas
Organic food and agriculture	• Soil health • Food waste • Sustainable fashion
Affordable and accessible healthcare	• Maternal and child health • Disease prevention and response • Mental and spiritual health • Health technology
Homelessness	• Job training and employment • Affordable housing • Financial inclusion and literacy
No poverty	• Investing in economic development • Social entrepreneurship • Refugees • Reduced inequalities
Gender lens investing	• Sweatshop and child labor • Reproductive rights and sexual health • Fem tech
Black Lives Matter	• Investments in black fund managers • Savings accounts in a black-owned bank • People of color on corporate boards • Investments in businesses run by people of color • Funding research around bias
Sustainable cities	• Urban revitalization • The future of mobility • Green buildings • Affordable housing
Animal welfare	• Cruelty-free businesses • Plant-based food companies

This is a high-level view—and as such, it might feel somewhat abstract. To make this more real, I will use myself as an example. My personal mission statement is to contribute to justice in communities that have been structurally excluded and to be responsible with my consumption. The vision I foresee as an outcome of my efforts is a more equitable global society that also thrives in nature rather than destroying it and bearing the consequences. While these are big goals, they align with the following areas of focus across my work, portfolio goals, consumer choices, how I view myself as a citizen, and even in my art collection. Knowing that my goals are much larger than myself, I have mapped my own desire for change to the following SDGs:

- No poverty (Goal 1)
- Quality education (Goal 4)
- Gender equality (Goal 5)
- Affordable and clean energy (Goal 7)
- Reduced inequalities (Goal 10)
- Responsible consumption and production (Goal 12)
- Climate action (Goal 13)
- Peace, justice, and strong institutions (Goal 16)

At Beyond Capital, our vision is to sustainably increase the quality of life and standard of living for consumers at the bottom of the economic pyramid, and our mission is to sustainably support early-stage social enterprises throughout India, Kenya, Tanzania, Rwanda, and Uganda. In doing so, we are dedicated to being the first professional investment capital invested into a social enterprise—providing management advisory, pro bono resources, and mentoring to ensure the company's success—and to being a long-term partner to help our portfolio companies maintain fidelity to their social missions.

The Beyond Capital portfolio's goal is to align with the following SDGs:

- No poverty (Goal 1)
- Zero hunger (Goal 2)
- Good health and well-being (Goal 3)
- Gender equality (Goal 5)
- Decent Work & Economic Growth (Goal 8)
- Reduced Inequalities (Goal 10)
- Responsible Consumption & Production (Goal 12)
- Partnerships for the Goals (Goal 17)

Out of over a dozen investments, every company contributes to Goals 1, 2, and 5, with individual companies reaching toward the other goals we track toward.

Even though my personal and professional goals are outlined as such, when considering your own areas of focus, do not worry too much about being fully aligned with the SDGs. As the current gold standard of criteria for how investors can track their values against global goals, they are no doubt a useful framework. Accordingly, they can be a great tool to help you define your values and measure your investments against. However, if you are clear on what you want to focus on and it is not listed as an SDG, that is an equally valid approach.

examine your implicit biases

Arlan Hamilton built every inch of her venture fund career by taking a road that no one has traveled. Today, she is the founder and managing partner of Backstage Capital, which invests in BIPOC, women, and LGBTQ+ founders. In the context of investing her background is untraditional. According to Hamilton, there are many well-intentioned investors who want to be more equitable but who may prevent themselves from doing so because they feel compelled to follow the conventional path, or the status quo. In considering whether there is a universal element of her due diligence process that would help create a more inclusive culture around investing, Hamilton admits that, like most investors, she herself is often pattern-matching in her own due diligence—though she has a different pattern from which to match. That pattern is often centered on her view of a middle-aged, multitasking Black woman—the group of women she identifies with the most and whom she holds up as personal heroes. She saw them as the default and able to perform. Hamilton would also like to contribute to a new set of rules and guidelines, even if they are unspoken in venture due diligence to even the playing field. She believes that she possesses an advantage because she does not have to train herself to think or see differently—because that is already how she sees the world.[69]

In 2020, I transitioned from the "buy side" (where I was the investor) to the "sell side" (where I was pitching a venture fund product to investors). In doing that, I realized some of the biases that may have been influencing our rigorous due diligence, which is rooted in the practices of traditional finance. Luckily, I have colleagues who have constantly pushed the impact investing community to think differently about how they evaluate companies in order to allow for greater diversity, and I am learning how to account for these biases.

However, now that I am on the other side of the table, I have become impacted by the bias of others. From this vantage, I have observed how more traditional investors have entrenched biases around how much money a fund manager is investing into her fund and whether *they* decide to legitimize a long-standing track record if it was under a nontraditional structure like Beyond Capital. When I would speak about the market opportunities to invest in low-income populations (a market of over a billion people where we invest), many investors would immediately gloss over and shy away from the investment without truly evaluating the opportunity simply because of their deeply held beliefs, while other investors thought differently and sought to understand the investment case for innovations around basic goods and services for consumers living on less than fifteen dollars per day.

It is often said that we do not know what we do not know. It is equally true that we do not know what we *unconsciously* know—in other words, our implicit biases. Implicit bias is an unconscious attribution of particular qualities to a member of a certain group. Once you become aware of this concept, it can be a useful tool to help you explore your own values, where they came from, and how they might have formed. After all, each of us views our environment through our own particular lens, which is shaped by the information and opinions that we have been exposed to. Not only are these opinions and this information often transmitted by individuals with their own biases, but they also work to form our own. To examine your values through a more objective lens, then, it is important you take your own implicit biases into account.

As a start, implicit bias can relate to race, gender, socioeconomics, ageism, and ableism, just to name a few possible examples. Issues related to implicit bias often have to do with the perceived merit of a particular group and their ability to perform relative to a preconceived standard. Most of us do not *want* to prejudge a person or a group based on our own bias, but we often do—precisely because we are not aware that these biases exist.

The signs of bias are everywhere once you know where to look. For instance, a person with autism has traditionally been viewed as unable to fully function within society. Now that more thought has been given to the systems in which those with autism can live and thrive, schools, jobs, and other incredible opportunities have arisen to better accommodate those individuals who have autism spectrum disorder.

Another example would be the presence and roles of women in Silicon Valley. While the culture was not intentionally built to disadvantage women, that has nevertheless been the result. Deep-rooted implicit biases lead many men to believe that women are not as good at math or science, or that they are too emotionally fragile to thrive in the fast-paced, high-pressure environments of the typical tech startup. *Au contraire.*

In more recent years, many Silicon Valley companies have begun taking more positive steps to recognize biases in their hiring practices and other company policies and to address the issues that stem from them. An example of a fund that is proactively working to narrow the bias gap in the tech sector is the venture capital fund Kapor Capital. Kapor Capital invests in tech-driven early-stage companies committed to closing gaps of access, opportunity, or outcome for low-income communities and communities of color in the United States. The fund thinks of its impact as leveraging information technology to solve real-world problems and improve lives. Driving this effort is the company's commitment to diversity, as reflected by both their internal teams and the entrepreneurs they work with. Kapor Capital believes that the lived experience of founding teams from underrepresented backgrounds provides a competitive edge. Their experiences inform the questions they ask and the problems they identify that give rise to profitable tech-driven solutions.[70]

Companies like Kapor Capital help to highlight the problems of unconscious bias—specifically, that thinking on the surface level about what our values are might not be enough. By pushing yourself to go deeper inside, by working to see where your own biases might lie, you can learn to recognize and push beyond them and better refine and understand the impact you hope to make.

This kind of transformative work is critical to the social change that we need today, and for that reason, it should be considered an ongoing effort. As I write this in 2020, against the backdrop of the deaths of too many Black Americans and the growing visibility of the Black Lives Matter movement, I know personally that it is more important than ever for me to spend time thinking about where my implicit biases are, whether they lie along racial, gender, or socio-economic lines. By understanding those biases, I can better understand how I am holding myself back from achieving deeper levels of impact.

taking action

One of the places where I believe I can have a strong impact is engaging others so that impact investing becomes more than just a niche industry. At the many dinner tables I have sat at over the past decade, the majority of those seated around me have had little concept of what impact investing was. Despite having both the ability and the means to live a life in which their money was more aligned with their values, they feel detached from the many challenges facing the world, they do not see them as related to their lives, and therefore, they do not prioritize impact when making their investment decisions. This is both frustrating and worrying (and a primary driver of why I set out to write this book).

To tap into this passion, I operate as an entrepreneur in the impact investment space. I travel frequently to give talks and organize events all with the goal of solving a very basic pain point: lack of awareness. One of the primary ways I do this is through the Beyond Capital Ambassador Program. For a reasonable annual donation, ambassadors have access to exclusive content, networking events, and engagement with entrepreneurs. Ambassadors are also invited to join us on the ground for site visits to India and East Africa, so they can get to know our portfolio companies and tap more directly into the power of impact investing. As of this writing, we have fifty-five ambassadors in fourteen cities around the world.

In 2019 alone, the year I was pregnant with my daughter, I convened or was a speaker at twenty-four events! I do not say this to show off but to illustrate the tremendous energy I have found by living according to my values.

I have also launched a podcast, with my cohost Ed Stevens, a seasoned entrepreneur and executive and the CEO of Preciate, a B Corporation dedicated to helping professionals build relational wealth (notice this is another type of wealth). I look up to Ed for the clarity he brings to business with purpose and the way he runs Preciate. I am fascinated by his concept of relational wealth and how he works to relate credible, portable, and enduring examples of career accomplishments.

Through working with Ed on our podcast, I have been able to widen Beyond Capital's audience even further—and not just with my experience but with the stories of other purpose-driven leaders from across the globe.

When I spoke with Carrie Freeman of Second Muse, she shared about her belief in the Baha'i faith, which is a religion just 160 years old. Baha'i's overarching message is one of unity and equality, believing that humanity is capable of doing more, especially from a moral, ethical, and spiritual perspective. I knew about the faith because my husband and his family are Baha'is, and the faith has played a role in my life. Second Muse is founded by Baha'is, and Carrie's role helps her clients—such as NASA and Nike—design more inclusive business. The company emphasizes the concept of inclusive growth that considers all stakeholders. This mission is in direct alignment with Carrie's own religious values, making it incredibly fulfilling and rewarding work.[71]

Then, there was Jessica Bailey, who worked on climate change and clean energy at the Rockefeller Brothers' fund. In 2015, after almost ten years with that organization, she started her own firm, Greenworks Lending. Jessica's firm provides financing for commercial real estate properties to improve their energy consumption and renewable energy infrastructure, structured so that owners can pay back their loan as part of their property taxes. This makes borrowing more palatable and renewable energy more accessible. Because Jessica used her background in policy to inform her new business model, large-scale commercial real estate owners can become greener, which has a massive impact on the environment as a whole.[72]

Another entrepreneur I interviewed, Rick Perez, has created the world's largest recycling company—Avangard Innovative. His business model helps other companies optimize and monetize their garbage through corporate waste recycling programs, and he also encourages the specific recycling of items like plastic wrap, which cannot be recycled easily. By setting the ultimate goal of contributing to a circular economy, he encourages the recycling of these odd products for repeat use within the business.

Positive impact is an important part of his approach, but it goes well beyond recycling. As an immigrant himself, Rick believes it is important to hire people from different backgrounds. He is constantly giving back to his own community and the environment—from working toward zero waste on site to establishing health clinics and daycares around his facilities.

In theory, anyone can start a recycling company. In practice, Rick was able to start a recycling company based on his specific values, which enabled him to work toward ambitious and holistic goals and see them come to fruition.[73]

These examples are just a few of the remarkable conscious leaders I have come to know and be inspired by, each living out their values in significant ways. Because of their clarity of purpose, they see ways to move the needle in everything they do—and that is something anyone can do.

playing your role

Once you have a sense of your values, the big question then becomes where do you start? What role can you play in solving a problem that is so much bigger than yourself? Here are some questions to help you get started:

- How can I be aligned with my values?
- What are the needs of the communities who anchor me?
- What can I offer my full energy?
- What is my position in the movement and my personal scope of influence?

This last question is particularly important, as it helps you hone in on the role you want to occupy within the area that you plan to focus on with your resources. As Jasmine Rashid, Director of Advocacy and Strategic Partnerships at Candide Group, wrote, there are different roles to play within movements. Looking for change with your resources, you may be able to have a greater impact by thinking about what your role is.

Rashid outlines ten different roles, each describing a type of person you have likely met and worked with in your own life. For example, there are weavers, those who see through-lines of connectivity between people, places, organizations, ideas, and movements. Then, there are visionaries, who imagine and generate the boldest possibilities, hopes, and dreams and remind us of our direction. And, of course, we cannot forget the builders, who develop, organize, and implement ideas, practices, people, and resources in service of a collective vision.[74] I think of myself as a builder. By spending some time on your role and area of contribution, not only will you understand your own values better but also how you are valuable to the movement and how you can be an effective part of it.

embracing your authentic self

Imagine sitting down at a dinner party and immediately being able to connect over the different roles that each person plays in creating good in their communities. This would allow us to bring our most authentic selves to a unified conversation. I imagine a conversation that would not rest on the hierarchy of monetary wealth I have observed for my adult life—a conversation that, to be frank, has been missing for me. I want more. I want my peers to be a part of an active community around conscious investing, and I know it is possible.

In his book, *Solve for Happy*, one of my favorite Google engineers, Mo Gawdat, says humans are happiest when they strip away all their perceived selves. In a group of activated, aware impact investors, topics of conversation reach far beyond the oft-banal discussions of vacations, cars, and how to take advantage of the stock market or how to save on taxes. Those experiences of privilege come second to the expression of impact that we are able to create with our resources. They are coupled with vulnerability and honesty and have freed me and can free you from thinking you have to express yourself one certain way.

And for those who have defined their values well, these investments—of money, time, energy, and relationships—have never come at a better time in history. There have never been as many opportunities to address social problems as there are right now.

You might not naturally find yourself living exactly according to your values just yet, and that is perfectly fine. It is enough to know that this is a paradigm shift and a lifestyle that is available to you. Simply start—anywhere. As soon as you get the ball rolling, it will feel more natural, free, and even fun to be connected emotionally to your money and know that it is working in ways that make you feel good.

stakeholder capitalism

Most purpose-driven leaders practice what is known as *stakeholder capitalism*. In general, stakeholder capitalism breaks the paradigm of capitalism down to values more than just shareholder returns. The organization or company is oriented to serve the interest of *all* of their stakeholders—including customers, suppliers, employees, shareholders, and local communities.

Stakeholder capitalism has come to the forefront in more recent years. B Corporations, for instance, have designed their business models around the core concepts of stakeholder capitalism. In 2019, the Business Roundtable—a group of high-profile CEOs focused on the key issue areas of a strong economy—stressed the importance of stakeholder capitalism as a means of closing the advantage gap and addressing the growing threat of global climate change.[75] Even more recently, the COVID-19 pandemic has made clear that we still live in a culture as a whole that does not value all its stakeholders, with near daily reports of employees being mistreated, underpaid, and under-supported while being called to work in often life-threatening conditions.

Stakeholder capitalism matters for conscious investors because it offers an invaluable lens for looking at the root of the issues that you care about and want to solve. Thinking about all the stakeholders involved in your area of focus may be helpful in zeroing in on how you want to express your values in more specific ways.

At Beyond Capital, we have incorporated the philosophy of stakeholder capitalism into our evaluation process. We look at the stakeholders involved in all of our potential investments to ensure that these investments would be in line with our stated values. This process begins with a few basic questions:

- Who is benefitting and being positively impacted by the potential investment?
- Who or what might not benefit or be unexpectedly impacted by a proposed investment?

For instance, say that one of your areas of focus for doing good is healthcare. Ask yourself:

- Why do you care about this specific area?
- Is it because you care about patient access to affordable healthcare?
- Or rather, is it because you would like to contribute to a more robust and coordinated national healthcare system that can better manage global pandemics?
- Is it because you care about creating world-class, life-changing drug research facilities? And, in doing so, would you think about the carbon footprint of a global vaccine roll out or better workplaces for researchers?

By thinking deeper about the problem you want to contribute to solving, you begin to see the many different directions you can focus your efforts—and who or what might be impacted as a result. If you are focused on better patient outcomes, for instance, you may be interested in investing in a manufacturer of medical equipment. However, if you also incorporate environmental impact into your approach, then you will want to look into how that manufacturer operates and whether, by helping one stakeholder (the patients), you are harming another (the many individuals affected by an unhealthy environment).

mapping your core attributes

In 2020, I took part in a workshop intended to help me identify and understand my core attributes, and then to create an action plan to integrate those attributes into my life. It was at a time in my life where I was trying to not only invest and use my money to do good but also to align my whole life with the idea of doing good.

After listing out my values, I found a striking connection between my attributes and how they mapped directly to the investment thesis of Beyond Capital, as the following table demonstrates:

Core Attribute	Correlation to Beyond Capital
Abundance	Our belief that change is possible and that there can be more to a system than what is currently there. The belief that the pie can grow.
Authenticity	Our mission to invest in founders committed to conscious leadership and to meet the needs of the communities lacking access to basic goods and services.
Curiosity	Our willingness to think beyond what is and ask ourselves what *could* be.
Empathy	Our emphasis on caring about the people behind our investments and recognizing that we are all in this effort together.
Fun	Our belief that everything we do, even the most serious undertaking, should possess an element of fun.

Innovation	Our effort to use creativity, innovation, and technology to push the boundaries of what is possible.
Justice	Our commitment to investing in structural inequality and biased financial systems in order to foster greater fairness in capitalism.
Leadership	Our desire to show that a leader, what she believes in, and how she communicates—to employees, to stakeholders, and to customers—really does matter.
Purpose	Our focus on bringing purpose to our daily activities and to inspire the same desire for purpose in the companies in our portfolio.
Service	Our emphasis on thinking about more than just the financial bottom line.
Whole-heartedness	Our desire to act also from empathy, kindness, and patience in our work, leading us to invest in a way that is motivated by more than just financial return.

Seeing these attributes listed out and the impact they already had on my life was quite revealing. Nobody had ever asked me to identify what I considered the core attributes of myself, let alone consider how they contributed to the impact I created as a conscious investor.

Because I know the impact this exercise had on me, I encourage you to try it as well. What are your core attributes? How do they correlate with your values and to the efforts you are already involved in?

what legacy will you leave?

As you can see by the many and varied discussions in this chapter, there can be a lot to consider when working to define your values.

Any one of these considerations can make an excellent starting point. However, ultimately, the most crucial consideration when defining your values is your heart—which is why I put such an emphasis on wholeheartedness when considering my own core attributes.

According to author Brené Brown, as we moved from the twentieth into the twenty-first century, the heart was taken out of our leadership—which has led to some challenges. If we are to dare to lead, as Brown likes to say, then we must remember that we must bring our whole selves—our whole hearts—to the process. As much as you can, think about your values from the perspective of your heart, and not just your head.

Think as well about the legacy that you want to leave. When you think about business, business leaders, and the role they have in society, some may not believe in purpose-driven leadership, but nearly all of them have children or employees and want to leave behind a positive legacy.

No matter who you are, whether you have children, employees, or a close network of friends or peers, most likely you also want to leave a legacy of your own, to put a stamp on the future by contributing to the success of future generations. If none of the other approaches or considerations in this chapter resonate with you, I encourage you to think about the legacy you want to leave. Look through the lens of the company you want to leave behind for your employees or the world you want to leave behind for your children. How do you want them to remember your time on this earth?

When I published this book, I was thirty-six years old. I was raising my second venture fund and had already been reaching over seven million lives with the first fund. I was just getting started. I want my legacy to be about being an inclusive investor, having backed many different types of entrepreneurs with incredible ideas that produced financial and social results—and having truly changed lives with access to basic goods and services.

Another person who inspires me when I think of the concept of legacy is Suzanne Biegel, who has pioneered the gender lens investing movement around the globe. I have personally sat at dinner tables with Biegel in Los Angeles, London, and Delhi, where she shows up with the purpose to shed light on how women are an opportunity to invest in and what the benefits of investing in women will be for everyone on the planet. For Biegel, her legacy is not about recognition for her efforts but for the cause. To her, legacy is about being a "catalyst at large," to spark movements wherever she goes. She has inspired me to think differently about my own legacy.

CHAPTER 6

practice wealth consciousness

Lisa Kleissner worked in Silicon Valley as an architect. She and her husband, Charly, accumulated wealth from an exit from a tech company as well as from architect projects she had worked on. When Lisa started investing her capital around the turn of the century, she and her husband felt strongly that they were not the sole stewards of their capital. Today, Lisa is adamant that she is not interested in investing unless one or more forms of impact are part of the conversation. But it took time and intentionality to reach that point, especially since impact investing opportunities were not as available as they are today.

Lisa grew up in Hawaii, where her dad had a small medical supply business. He was an incredibly generous man, often giving free help and support to the many Medicaid and Medicare patients who needed his products to enhance their lives. At one point, he had accumulated an outstanding account receivable to the State of Hawaii. The company's debt came from the way he had helped the community. To solve the problem, he had to find a way to take out a bridge loan.

Lisa was fourteen when her father met with the bank. Although he laid out all the evidence and explained his situation, the bank refused to give him a loan.

Lisa remembered walking out of the meeting in awe of the incredible power the banker had. If he knew his decision was going to cause so many families so much grief, would he still have made the same decision? Did he even know what was behind it? In many ways, Lisa's story foreshadowed modern society, where large corporations exert a heavy influence on both our economy and on our lives.

Ultimately, Lisa's dad had to sell his business, and he used the assets to benefit a tiered structure of people, creating a sustainable business as well as providing services for those who had fallen out of the healthcare system because of their lack of insurance. He may have experienced setbacks, but he was still committed to creating a system that addressed the needs of his community.

In today's terms, Lisa's father's philosophy resembles the philosophy of stakeholder capitalism discussed previously. Lisa grew up with a distrust of banks and the financial system. She became skeptical about investments, and while she and her husband began building their investment portfolio at the turn of the century, she endeavored to think differently about her interactions with the financial system.

Early on, Lisa and Charly wanted to reassess how to invest their wealth. Inspired by an ad for a particular credit card that donated a percentage of customer spending to environmental organizations, Lisa decided that everything they did with their capital could have a benefit beyond the immediate. They began to ask bold questions of their investment advisor, insisting that their money should create measurable and positive good for specific communities. Until they knew exactly what their money would affect, they put a hold on all of their investing.

Since that discovery period, Lisa has continuously aligned her values with her money. She now has a number of her own portfolios that address different financial and impact needs. Additionally, she and Charly have come together with other impact investors to co-found Toniic and establish Hawaii Investment Ready, a nonprofit business accelerator that helps small businesses become stronger. Lisa also sits on the board of an investment fund called Aqua-Spark, which invests in sustainable aquaculture, addressing Lisa's support for ocean conservation, which has been a value Lisa has held since her childhood growing up in Hawaii.

All of Lisa's choices stem from her belief that her money is not her own—her belief that it is a public good. She also believes in deep impact as a mindset to inspire values-alignment in all areas of life. She has inspired me and many others to think about aligning all our money, time, and resources with our intention to do good.

It was not easy for Lisa to make this shift. Lisa experienced a lot of frustration and walked out of many meetings when the occasion called for it. Even now, if an advisor has no recommendations for Lisa, she puts her foot down and challenges their paradigm. Lisa believes that the years between 2020 and 2025 are pivotal and that the investment industry needs to act more in order to have opportunities to invest with a conscience—or consciously—that are genuine and authentic, rather than superficial. In her words, it is not just about getting to 100 percent of aligned impact investments in a portfolio. It is about getting to a *meaningful* 100 percent.

Impact investing has existed in many forms over the years, but the recent wave of wealth holders like Lisa have shaped the scene into what it is today: a tangible way to practice wealth consciousness, own your values, and do good.

no investment is neutral

It is human nature to want to feel good, be at ease, and to act in ways that inspire you and others around you. But how often are you encouraged to connect those emotions to your money? Based on the reactions I observe from conversations with investors, this concept is not something that is discussed enough. At every single talk I give, at least one person approaches me to say that the concept of their money having emotional value was new to them. In fact, why *do we not* think about what more our money can do?

That is what wealth consciousness is all about: knowing where your money and consumer choices are having an impact, in both positive and negative ways.

Remember, there is no such thing as a neutral investment. From the products you buy at the supermarket to the composition of your investment portfolio or retirement savings, everything you do with your money has some kind of impact. Yet, without practicing wealth consciousness, we are blind to the deeper impact and unable to align with our values. Going back to the concept of stakeholder capitalism, a simple exercise is to ask if where you put your money works for all stakeholders involved—that is, for an organization's employees, customers, suppliers, management, and shareholders.

But investments have never been just about the return, even if extenuating impacts are only considered as an afterthought. Investing in a traditional oil company will likely provide some positive financial growth, but the environmental cost of that return and supporting a fossil fuel company over the long term will likely be significant. Each of us has a responsibility to consider the real value behind every dollar we spend.

That process begins by asking some more basic questions: what is the purpose of money, and why do we have it?

The simple explanation is that money helps us take care of our basic needs—it helps to feed us and to put a roof over our heads. But that explanation does not even come close to scratching the surface, and at least parts of your answer may be wholly subjective. When practicing wealth consciousness, it is important that you examine these answers and what they mean to you. Once you have an understanding of what the purpose of your money is, you will be able to move forward with strength.

INFORMATION AVOIDANCE

As humans, we have a tendency to avoid information that can help us make decisions or is important despite evidence. The science is spelled out in David DiSalvo's book, *What Makes Your Brain Happy and Why You Should Do the Opposite*. Practically, as humans, we ignore what makes us uncertain or uncomfortable, which can be information about our investments that we are scared or worried about.

The best example of how information avoidance plays out in investing is climate change. George Marshall's work and book, *Don't Even Think About It*, is centered on the question of whether or not we are hardwired to deny climate change. Drawing on a wide range of social science research to explain why it is natural for us as a species to prefer not to think about climate change and its implications (and even to not coordinate a response), the short answer is, "No." However, psychological hindrances to accepting climate change and grasping its critical nature are nevertheless a legitimate issue we need to address.

Marshall also picks up on a number of psychological phenomena, including terror management theory, cognitive bias, and the bystander effect—all leading to information avoidance and complacency. In his interviews with a wide range of voices in the climate change debate from scientists to skeptics, the conclusion remains that the major climate change challenge before us is not scientific or technical but psychological.

This matters because climate change is the E in ESG, and DiSalvo and Marshall's work translates to why investors may be resistant to knowing what they own and taking the steps to care enough about investing consciously.

While it is up to us to decide what we take seriously (even though, as a species, humans will always prefer certainty), we must accept that uncertainty is at the frontiers of knowledge, some that require urgent solutions. The need to find an emotional connection to our money is grounded in science because humans need to conceptualize something emotionally in order to act on it.[76] The World Economic Forum's 2018 risk report highlights the failure of climate change mitigation and adaptation as one of the most impactful and probable issues facing the global economy, and the Financial Stability Board asserts that climate is "the most significant risk investors face."

But in a 2017 CFA Society ESG survey, only 50 percent of respondents admitted incorporating environmental issues into their investment process, and the main reason cited was immateriality.[77]

What is it going to take for you to want to become more active and respond?

FIND OUT WHAT YOU OWN

Global stock markets are the most ubiquitous markets for investment, yet they are often made to feel impersonal and detached from anything but their growth or decline over time. Typically, investors invests in the stock market through mutual funds or exchange-traded funds that someone else manages. For example, a retail investor with a retirement savings or an investment portfolio, small or large, will invest that capital in funds rather than have individual stocks picked for them. These are more cost-effective ways of investing because it is more efficient for a client advisor to rely on a team fund manager rather than select individual stocks themselves for each client's needs. The problem is that an investor may not always know what funds contain.

A typical exchange-traded fund (ETF) is weighted toward specific assets or market indices but not necessarily toward specific values. Imagine that you want to track the broad markets, including the S&P 500, Dow Jones, or NASDAQ. But what if it includes companies with values or practices that do not align with your own? You are powerless to change that—other than to not invest in that fund.

If you are reading this book, chances are that you have felt that sense of powerlessness in the traditional model of investing. You also know now that this is not your only option. Life is a series of personal choices, and as an investor, your choices have broad effects on your surrounding environment. Investing the wrong way or not knowing what your money is doing is a personal choice as well—and these choices can have lasting consequences, as is evident when considering issues such as climate change or lack of diversity.

Many individuals lack an understanding of their ownership, yet it is not that hard to find out what you actually do own. Yes, you might need to do a little bit of investigation, but the stock and bond positions in your portfolio should be easy to ascertain.

If you have invested in the Vanguard Russell 1000 Index Fund, for instance, you can go to Vanguard's website and find a tear sheet that lists every stock in that fund. The top holdings of that fund usually include larger companies like Microsoft, Apple, Amazon, and Facebook. Once you have learned what stocks are underlying the funds that you own, ask yourself if you want to own those companies and give yourself permission to ask more detailed questions. While many technology companies score high on ESG, they may not meet all your values, and you should evaluate them on what matters to you.

It is always worth doing your research. Learn about how these companies behave, how they treat their employees, how many women and people of color they have in leadership positions, and how each company acts as a steward of the environment in their field. Then, look at these answers and ask yourself whether each company truly conducts itself in a way that is consistent with *your* values.

If you work with a client advisor, your portfolio might be more nuanced. In that instance, ask questions of your advisor. It can be that simple!

If you want to be invested in a fund that does not have a specific lens for screening out companies, recognize that you might be investing in areas that are *not* 100 percent consistent with your values. The good news is there are still a lot of options to invest with your values in mind out there. Take matters into your own hands. Be confident as you research the different investments in your portfolio and what they do (or do not) stand for. If you feel a little helpless at times in getting to the bottom of your investments, know that you are not alone but that the work is worth it in the end.

Options are expanding. By the time you read this book, there may be many more ways to align your values and investments quickly and affordably. Having faith that you will be able to achieve your investment goals is important when bringing your heart closer to your investments.

KNOW THE DEPTH OF YOUR IMPACT

In the next chapter, we will look at the markers of social and environmental impact that can help you invest with greater awareness and choice. But while a lot of those criteria are aspirational, conscious investing is certainly concerned with measuring actual impact now and into the future. How do you assess where your money is having an impact? Intuitively, you might want to measure the financial part of an investment by looking at the profit numbers alone. But the qualitative data can be just as important as it helps refer back to your values.

At Beyond Capital, we start first by cooperating with the founders of the companies we are evaluating to define the goals for each investment in line with our mission and determine what we want to measure. Then, measurement and tracking become a function of staying close to the investment. Data-driven companies are easier to track and produce regular business insights. Measuring the impact of investments into other companies requires a little more work. Once we have these metrics systems established, we compile the data from the monthly company reports and determine the number of individuals impacted by our portfolio, the number of women impacted by our portfolio, and the number of jobs created by our portfolio companies. By monitoring and measuring, we also ensure that we as investors, entrepreneurs, and operators do not lose sight of our own impact goals.

We also measure company-specific metrics since we invest in multiple sectors. One of the companies we have invested in is Numida, a financial inclusion business based in Uganda. Numida is a tech-enabled company that lends to small business owners because access to capital for small businesses is holding back development on the African continent. Small businesses account for 77 percent of all jobs in Africa and as much as half the GDP in some countries. Numida's first touch point with business owners is its app, which allows them to track their expenses and create a bookkeeping system. By systematizing often informally managed businesses and allowing users to accumulate two weeks of data, they unlock the ability to borrow money. The average loan size is $176, but business owners can start out with smaller loans. Each loan is short-term in duration and is typically repaid in two to three months. Shafique, one of Numida's borrowers who runs a small detergent manufacturing business, did not have the working capital needed to run his business after paying school fees for his daughter. Sadly, choosing between prosperity and education is not uncommon. But since Numida issued him a working capital loan, he has been able to take care of his family and grow his business.

Once a user repays their loan, they become entitled to borrow a larger amount. By repaying each of his loans, Shafique has been able to grow his credit limit—and his business—quickly.

To assess the impact of our investment in Numida, we measure:

- The number of borrowers to track the number of small and medium-sized enterprises that have had access to capital
- The number of female borrowers to track a focus on elevating female business owners
- The number of repeat borrowers to show interest in utilizing Numida's product long-term

- Average loan size to track how Numida's model is growing with their borrowers
- Number of total loans to track the overall magnitude of financial inclusion
- Jobs created by loans to show how loans are impacting business and enabling them to grow
- Users tracking expenses, which leads to increased financial literacy
- Users with insurance to show an increase in sophistication of the businesses they are lending to and their ability to think long-term
- Number of savings accounts to highlight the ability for borrowers to save for the future and for larger purchases like healthcare, education, and other areas that will improve their livelihood
- Percent of female savers to highlight how women are saving for the futures of their families

We also measure and track default rates of the loans as a means of measuring success of the business and their model. Beyond Capital's impact reporting framework tracks these impact results as well as the potential growth of the value of the investment. Our goal is to invest in passionate entrepreneurs, to fill the capital gap, and to ensure that companies have advisory support in bringing maturity and sophistication to an early-stage market. In our work, the gap in investment capital is characteristic of these early stages of funding, when a company is still perceived as a risky investment.

We want our portfolio companies to add value in the areas where they work, a concept also known as *additionality*. Additionality refers to the supplemental impact that was achieved by the conscious investment—which prompts the question of whether the positive impact would have been achieved even without the presence of the investment. We want our companies to have clear missions and well-defined goals. We want them to improve the lives of low-income people with access to goods and services. We want to invest in scalable and reliable companies that have a good reporting framework to measure, scale, and communicate their impact widely.

With designated factors to focus on when we find a new business, we already have a lens in place to assess, analyze, and measure the company's social impact. In the same way that we defined our values and determined our investment thesis ahead of our investments, we determine the results we want to see ahead of time in order to dictate our impact thesis. We call this a *theory of change.*

Investing in alignment with a defined theory of change is not just the purview of organizations like Beyond Capital and B Corporations. Anyone can do it. To get started, your first step would be to understand and define the impact data you want to measure before and after the investment is made.

Setting a baseline at the time you invest will help you measure your goals later on. In other words, measure the level of female leadership in the company when you invest. Once you have exited or sold the investment, you can look back on what impact you wanted to have at the start. Over time, for instance, perhaps that portfolio of investments held a hundred companies where women were key decision-makers within companies and in leadership positions, and those companies thrived. Aside from your return on your investment, you have also had the impact of being part of a movement that singles out and supports companies with women in leadership roles for the purpose of making money, doing good, and supporting a movement at the same time.

When we measure these factors, we get information about the company's overall performance. Is the company growing their number of borrowers? Is it increasing its average loan size? Are the total loans and jobs created increasing? By answering these questions, we can determine how the business is doing and what kind of impact it is creating. We may even be able to measure outcomes, positive actions, and consequences of these measurements. We can also identify mission drift.

There are other, more sophisticated ways to measure impact. One is through the Internet of Things and blockchain technology, which can generate and track data and also introduce verification systems so that investors can understand more deeply where their money is having impact.[78] At the time this book was published, we were piloting blockchain verification of impact in the Beyond Capital portfolio.

Even at home, there are other ways you and your family can measure your efforts. Hooman and I are quite fond of what are known as family planning meetings, in which we create a dashboard to help us visualize how we are contributing beyond our family. This tool is useful not only for measuring the change we are creating through our investments but also through our philanthropy, our time, other resources, and our networks and relationships. When Hooman and I can see what collectively we are working toward, not only does it strengthen our bond and show how we are working together, but it helps us understand our impact in a more holistic way.

Ultimately, hope does not require analysis, but it can be an important component of a social or environmental change agenda. It is important to define your theory of change and your desired impact; change will not come if we only value financial KPIs. Just like predicting the weather or assessing your job as a parent, there is a lot you can know, but some aspects will always remain unpredictable, especially when working within complex systems and important social and environmental problems that often intersect.

This is why hope is so important to civil rights lawyer and social justice advocate Bryan Stephenson. To Stephenson, effective change comes down to four key elements: one, get proximate; two, change the narrative; three, stay hopeful; and four, learn to be uncomfortable.[79]

These four steps do not measure specific indicators. However, as Stephenson says, if you want to make change, these are the behaviors that will make it happen.

Especially in the context of examining my own privilege, Stephenson's fourth point fascinates me. Many people often do not stop to consider what makes them uncomfortable and why. At a fundamental level, I believe that what separates those who believe their money can do good and those who do not is fear—specifically, the fear that they will lose out. If you believe that our society and our economy are a zero-sum game, then you also believe that you are losing when you are doing good. This is simply not the truth.

know your power

Just as important as the question of what you currently invest in, do not forget to ask yourself what you *can* invest in. You do have the power to invest in more, but if what is holding you back is measuring your impact, then my advice is this: get involved, learn how to start living in a way that is consistent with your values, and then you can start looking at the results of the impact you are having.

To be clear, measurement is important—but not so important that it should preclude action. Getting started is more important than having the "perfect" system for impact measurement beforehand. Do not make the mistake of using data as an excuse not to move forward. Instead, have the courage to take the first step, to change your behaviors in a positive way, and in so doing, learn how you can better quantify, qualify, and otherwise improve your efforts.

In other words, do not let perfect be the enemy of good. While I am typically very analytical in my approach to investing, I believe a lack of data should not stop you from making your first conscious investments. If you are investing directly into a company that does not have enough data, you may also be able to turn it into an opportunity to shape the company's behavior through active engagement with management or through shareholder voting.

Impact measurement has become a hot topic in the field of impact investing. With the old-school returns-first mindset still plaguing us, everyone wants to know exactly how effective investing in social and environmental outcomes can be and to what extent it is having an impact on the beneficiaries or the environment, the system in which the investment operates, and the potential negative consequence the investment creates. To become a conscious investor, a good starting point is simply to know what moves you. What do you want to change about your current investments? What impact do you want to have with your money and resources in the future?

The most important piece of all of this is to think carefully about the impact you want to have. Consider what a better world looks like to you and how your investment plays a role in that.

You can view your experiences and surroundings through one of two lenses: scarcity or abundance. Scarcity wants only measurable returns and is controlling over outcomes, while abundance knows that the good you do multiplies itself and trusts that impact is possible. Social and environmental impact is released when you unbound possibilities. Conscious investing is just one opportunity available to you in a mindset of abundance.

If you are feeling overwhelmed, remember that this is intended to be a positive process. Wealth consciousness and conscious investing fit into the mindset of abundance and serve us as complete, fulfilled people. You can also apply these mindsets to other areas in which you want to create impact. Step away from the pressure of getting it right, and instead, begin to get excited about the number of possibilities that open up to you when you align your financial life with your values.

CHAPTER 7

invest with awareness

Sometimes the decision *not* to do something is just as power-ful as the decision to do something. In mid-2007, I met with a hedge fund manager who was betting on the decline of subprime mortgages—also known as "the Big Short," a trade made famous by the 2015 movie of the same name—to hear his pitch.

One of the hedge fund managers who had identified the trade (not the one represented in the movie) reached out to my team with an invitation to tell us about his dedicated fund to invest in this one big idea. He described a "big, exciting idea" that he was going to create a completely dedicated fund for and called us into his office to discuss the details.

I will never forget that day. We were sitting across the conference table from one of the top hedge fund managers in New York City, listening to the pitch for the default of subprime mortgages, which were set to make them and their investors hundreds of millions of dollars in profit. The investment thesis was predicated on betting on the default of mortgages that were sold to home buyers who would not be able to afford them when the interest rates adjusted to a higher level. This strategy would create an incredible return for the investors in this fund.

As we walked out of the lavish office and took all thirty floors back to the ground level of a midtown building, we looked at each other with concern. The fund manager elaborated on how he would be making hundreds of millions of dollars off this investment. He was predicting the 2008 financial crisis and offering us the opportunity to make a return for our investors.

Here again, the zero-sum mentality can be seen at play. The fund manager's focus on profit came at the detriment of others—as if this was the only way to play the game—and perpetuated a deeply ingrained system of institutional racism. As American political strategist Heather McGhee points out, racism has a cost for everyone.[80] The common misconception is that everything toppled due to risky borrowers or people buying properties they could not afford, yet the majority of subprime mortgages went to home buyers with good credit history. Black and Latinx borrowers were three times as likely to be sold an adjustable-rate mortgage (ARM), and explanations of the ARM structure were often undertaken in bad faith. After the subprime mortgage crash, most of the nation's big lenders were fined for racial discrimination. One out of every five mortgages in the country was sold as an ARM. The crisis cost us *all* $19 trillion in lost wealth. The global economy would not have been forced to endure the financial crisis in 2008 were it not for these lending practices, rooted in racism.

Investing with awareness was not on my radar back then. I generally knew my social values, but I had not thought very deeply about how to invest my retirement savings or other investments to be consistent with them. What I had used most until this point was my voice and my network. I also learned while working in the asset management industry that you can be a steward of capital for different constituencies—including labor pension funds, which was the majority capital that we managed at my firm. As a result, my parents, who are extremely socially minded individuals, were less disappointed that I worked in the hedge fund industry and pointed out the impact we were having that initially was not on my radar.

But in the context of the Big Short, nobody was thinking deeply, especially about all stakeholders. This one investment was putting pressure on the banking system, pushing banks like Lehman Brothers to tip off the financial crisis. And all for a bet against buyers keeping their homes. (While these individuals likely would have lost their homes anyway and the mortgage brokers who sold them their mortgages were the genesis, the hedge fund manager that profited invested in products designed to amplify the impact of the defaults and make money.) It was a financial opportunity for a few dozen already very wealthy men who also led to the loss of jobs, pension funds, homes, and savings for countless innocent people. The Big Short was the exact opposite of investing with awareness.

While we did not invest in the dedicated fund that bet on the defaults of the adjustable-rate mortgages (because we were invested in the manager and the overall hedge fund), we had exposure to the Big Short and did profit for our investors. The fund itself made an impressive return when the financial crisis tipped off The Great Recession in 2008. And it was not hard to see the financial crisis coming after that day we heard about the Big Short trade. In fact, I spent hours thinking over where the shoe would drop knowing that the losses could be so great, and it ultimately did. After much obfuscation about exposure to subprime mortgages, on September 15, 2008, a day that stands sharply along with September 11 in my mind, Lehman Brothers filed for bankruptcy and the Bloomberg terminal on my desk flashed red as the company's stock plunged 93 percent in one day.

Today, my experience with the subprime mortgage trade reminds me of the importance of calling out unethical situations as they are happening, knowing how hard it can be to clean up the mess. While one could argue that the banking system creates opportunities for investors to take advantage of, in this specific case—credit default swaps, or insurance on the default of mortgages—I believe that I have a moral responsibility to act according to my values when making decisions, and you should too, when considering where to invest. One of the core attributes that guides my actions is justice. In retrospect, I would have been much prouder if we had been able to be honest about the true impact of that investment and how it could potentially damage the futures of certain stakeholders.

Wealth consciousness asks you to stay alert as you become entangled with investments and consumer choices. When you invest with awareness, you hold that consciousness through every portfolio update, pitch, and pivot. No investment is neutral—and it is up to you how to use that power.

toe dipping

Nothing I am laying out in this book needs to be viewed as extreme or absolute. We are simply creating a mindset shift that will help you make better decisions in the long run. Like me, you might get rid of your financial "plastic wrap" today, tomorrow, or in a year. And when you do, you will look at your environment differently. You will see the merit and great potential for good in your values and be able to bring them into your life in a more holistic way.

Toniic CEO Adam Bendell sees impact investing as a "rising tide" environment. To Bendell and other like-minded individuals, impact investing offers the opportunity to go beyond screening out investments to aligning your values and even running a business with integrity. In these ways, impact investors help to push the business sector far beyond what has been the norm in the past half-century or more.[81]

As your standards shift and you begin to look for investments that match your values, it is possible you may need to take a tiered approach to becoming a conscious investor. The first step likely would be screening out your investments for qualities that do not match your values. In the United States, the majority of investments are held in exchange-traded funds (ETFs). ETFs are funds that typically mirror exchanges, like the S&P 500, but in the case of environmental, social, and governance criteria, they are screened out for specific sectors that are not meeting social or environmental standards. While ETFs that apply ESG filters may provide more superficial impact, stopping on one level for a while does not mean you are only partially conscious. These are simply external markers that guide us through the network of conscious investing.

What does superficial mean? It means screening out for one or two particular areas but not thinking about the whole picture of the impact a company is having. It is not thinking about how that company is likely linked to a greater system of impact that goes beyond, for example, screening for female leadership and sound environmental practices.

If you have a greater risk tolerance, investing into impact-oriented venture capital, private equity, and real assets and directly into B Corporations and other socially conscious businesses could be right for your portfolio. I highly encourage you to work with an advisor to vet investments. As a full-time CEO, parent, wife, daughter, friend, and more, I have found that good investment advice is worth paying for.

With the help of an advisor, I am on a path toward a portfolio of more liquid investments that combine my personal passions for a more just world, workforce policies that promote diversity and inclusion, and to have in place strong and ethical governance measures, in addition to supporting companies that are conscious of their environmental footprint. I know that over time I can build out allocations to further direct impact in a way that works for my investment goals. As a part of my conscious investing strategy, I also support Beyond Capital and other organizations with philanthropic capital and time.

Remember, the starting point is often defining your values, discerning what impact you want to have, and setting your goals accordingly.

the advisor for you

There are many different types of financial advisors and ways they are compensated for their services. You can learn about financial advisors on your own without much effort. However, there are some considerations related to conscious investing that most of what you may find in your own research leaves out.

When thinking about choosing an advisor as it relates to conscious investing, the most important criteria is that they are aligned with your values, especially if you are on the path to becoming a conscious investor. Believe it or not, financial advisors can think about more than just money and have the ability to talk to you about more than just financial wealth.

A perfect example is Seth Streeter, Founder of Mission Wealth Partners, who believes in the nine dimensions of wealth for his clients: impact, emotions, relationships, fun, physical, spiritual, intellectual, career, and, finally, financial. Streeter helps his clients meet traditional goals like building their dream house, but as an advisor, he also makes sure they are fulfilled in these other dimensions. In these ways, Streeter serves as the perfect example of a financial advisor who does more—and he is not alone.[82]

Another example is Jennifer Kenning, who I mentioned previously and who works exclusively on social and environmental impact implementation for individual, foundation, corporate, and family office portfolios. To perform this work, Kenning has developed a strategy that helps clients outline the type of impact they want to have, understand the resources they have at their disposal (e.g., investments, grants, or time), and form a plan for thoroughly targeting resources to the problems or interests that they are best suited to solve. As further evidence that Kenning walks the talk, she also operates as a certified B Corporation—and as she likes to say, she was the first one out there to travel with her own reusable water bottle.[83]

It may take a little bit of work finding the right fit, but there are many advisors (mostly independent) who speak the language of conscious investing. Generally, independent registered investment advisors tend to have more control over the types of products and investment offerings that they recommend to you, and they tend to bring more heart to the work that they do. If you are considering investing with larger institutions, do what you can to fully investigate their values to determine whether they are walking the talk in all areas before moving forward.

It is also acceptable to interview your potential advisor, get to know them personally, learn what drives them, and get to know some of their team members before moving forward. In fact, before choosing an advisor, interview at least two or three different individuals to see who might be the best fit.

UNPACKING ESG

As previously discussed, ESG stands for *environmental, social, or governance factors*, which can be the lens through which investments, company operations, and risk factors are viewed. Screening for these factors ensures that standards with regard to environmental, social, or governance practices are upheld. If companies do not meet specific ESG requirements, they can be excluded from an ESG portfolio.

ESG screening is not new. For centuries, multiple religions and philosophies have had similar practices to what would be considered ESG governance today. Modern ESG can trace its roots to the United Nations. Filled with passionate advocates for global education and sustainability, in 2004, the United Nations invited more than fifty global industry leaders to discuss pressing ESG issues. These oftentense discussions led to a report called *Who Cares Wins*, which provided a compelling thesis on the value of ESG. This report directly led to the founding of the UN-backed Principles for Responsible Investment, a framework that works to encourage professional investors to consider ESG.[84]

In general, ESG funds have made impact investing more accessible, encouraging people to invest in companies that are considering these essential impact factors, mostly through elimination based on risk. ESG is not always about direct value creation or catalyzing action for social change goals. ESG funds typically employ environmental screens to gauge how a company performs as a steward of nature, social measurements to assess how a company manages relationships with all its stakeholders, and governance screens to assess how a company manages issues such as leadership, diversity and inclusion policies, executive pay, audits, internal controls, and shareholder rights. The challenge with ESG is that companies often self-report their progress in these three areas and may not be meeting all criteria to be included in your portfolio. Increasingly, ratings firms are digging deeper, but this is why your own due diligence is important, either through an advisor or your own research. With your values as a guide, you can create a set of questions that allows you to have a north star for your conscious investing compass.

Most all funds have descriptions on their fact sheets, detailing their investment strategy and top companies in the portfolio. While this due diligence may be time consuming, knowing what you own is a key aspect of wealth consciousness. There are also plenty of mostly independent advisors who have precise expertise in impact investing that could match your goals. ESG funds can be a good starting point for new impact investors, especially investors who need more liquid portfolios. Once you establish portfolio goals, you can then identify places where you would like to go even deeper. Every investor places a different emphasis on the depth of their impact. Some are hands on and prefer to engage with funds and socially-oriented companies more personally—they know who their fund managers are and offer mentorship to the CEOs and founders they invest in or sit on boards. Others prefer a more passive approach. My personal portfolio was the starting point for impact in my life, but my husband and I have selected an advisor we love who will help us make decisions in the decades to come so that we can run our organizations, spend time with our family and friends, and look for other ways that we can continue to integrate our values into our whole lives. If we are pursuing what Streeter refers to as the nine dimensions of wealth, then we have many avenues to continue to integrate our values into our life together.

WEIGHING YOUR OPTIONS

Recently, I spoke with an investor who had his own family office. He had recently been presented with the opportunity to invest in a business, and he liked the founder and was excited about the mission. As he told me about it, I saw a younger version of myself in him. The business did not seem like a great investment, but because he did not have the time to carry out his own research, he relied on a gut feeling or emotional connection to make his decision. Generally speaking, gut feelings, or emotions alone, are not the best way to allocate your money. And unless you have direct startup investing or operating experience, you may not want to start out with a portfolio of angel investments at first.

Impact investors have a higher duty to conduct comprehensive due diligence when weighing an investment opportunity. Conscious investors are not merely allocating resources to the business with the most viable financial potential but to the most feasible solution to a serious social, environmental, governance, or technological problem. Conscious investors should be aware that there are skeptics who might be looking to preserve an old system and are unwilling to acknowledge investment strategies that produce financial, social, and environmental returns, and therefore, you should take on the responsibility of choosing your investments wisely.

While becoming conscious about your choices is not complicated, choosing individual investments on your own can require work, and that is okay. Some of the most rewarding experiences and accomplishments in my life have taken time and patience. At Beyond Capital, we review and discuss about two hundred companies a year, and we only invest in a handful of those annually. Our portfolio had twelve investments at the time of publishing this book and impacted over seven million individuals living at low-income levels. If someone had told me that I was going to average over half a million people impacted per year when I set out to become a conscious investor, I would not have believed in the possibility of the good my money could do. But now that the results are proven, I know that creating a framework that includes your values and a clear set of expectations and maintaining a commitment to asking questions can yield both financial return and positive impact. And, as time goes on, there will be more opportunities to invest and improve at investing consciously.

In the meantime, small but intentional steps can go a long way toward bringing your money in alignment with your values. In fact, as challenging as this might sound, if you do not have a traditional client advisor or traditional banking relationship, you may actually have an easier time investing with awareness. One reason for this is that the banking and wealth management systems are built around traditional fiduciary duty and shareholder primacy. This means that financial institutions believe they have the obligation to serve the financial benefit of shareholders as their number-one priority. Investing online or through brokerage houses is acceptable as well and can eventually be tailored toward impact. In liquid assets (e.g., stocks and bonds), most online advisors offer sustainable investment solutions, though the way these solutions are advertised will depend on the platform. Industry experts have noted that State Street and Invesco are more carefully integrating impact into their investment strategies than their competitors. Be patient and thorough as you explore your options.

This book does not constitute investment advice. The following are a few general examples intended solely to highlight specific categories of impact investments and are for illustration purposes only. These examples are not intended to substitute for professional investment advice, professional financial advice, or general counsel. Please consult your financial advisor.

Public Securities

- **Socially responsible ETFs:** including iShares MSCI KLD 400 Social ETF, the Guggenheim S&P Global Water Index ETF, Aspiration Redwood Fund, Domini Impact International Equity Fund, and Pax MSCI EAFE ESG Leaders Index. Pax Ellevate Global Women's Leadership Fund is a mutual fund investing in four hundred listed companies with the most favorable gender leadership characteristics. Investors should also look for public-market options that offer other diversity filters.

- **Ellevest:** investing in women mostly through public markets, although the firm has a wealth management division. In Ellevest portfolios, investors can also select a partial impact investing option. Ellevest also provides loans to women-owned businesses and community services and invests in companies working to meet higher sustainability and ethics standards. The firm is headed by Wall Street veteran Sallie Krawcheck, who witnessed all the downfalls of investing without awareness firsthand.

More Direct and Active

These options are likely solely for accredited investors and have higher minimums:

- **Calvert Impact Capital Community Investment:** a debt investment firm that invests in a portfolio of funds that finance purpose-driven organizations with a long track record.

- **CNote:** CNote helps promote small business growth and job creation in underprivileged communities. Every dollar invested into CNote gets loaned out to female and minority enterprises to create affordable housing or bring opportunity to low-income areas.

- **Open Invest:** An investment advisor where investors can invest their entire portfolio or set up separately managed accounts tailored to causes.

- **Open Road Impact Fund:** This fund provides short-term bridge loans to social impact organizations that run into expected obstacles on their path to scale located across the globe.

- **Truss Fund:** This fund also provides emergency loans for purpose-driven businesses, where investors commit $10,000 as a recoverable grant. It is connected to a well-known, longstanding accelerator program in Silicon Valley.

- **Opportunity Fund Small Business Impact Fund:** This fund invests in small businesses, offering two- and five-year terms with a nominal spread over the benchmark U.S. Treasury interest rate. Over five years, the money they have raised will provide more than $38 million in loans for small businesses, create and retain more than 3,700 jobs, and generate $75 million in annual economic activity.

Conscious investing does not require you to invest millions up front. Even $100 can be invested consciously by being put into socially responsible funds.

GOING DEEPER

If you have a larger investment portfolio, you likely have more flexibility and access to a greater universe of investments. Think about more private investment options, such as private equity or venture capital, which will potentially allow for your impact to be more targeted and specific. You can also likely better implement a thematic approach, tackling one specific issue or focus area with all your assets, through funds that are mostly all available only to accredited investors. To give you a better idea of what this might look like, here are three examples:

- **Aqua-Spark** is a global investment fund that makes investments in sustainable aquaculture businesses that generate investment returns. At the time of publishing, Lisa Kleissner sat on the board of Aqua-Spark.

- **Impact Engine**'s mission is to bring more capital to a market where financial returns are linked to positive social and environmental impacts. Impact Engine manages funds for institutions and individuals that invest in for-profit, positive-impact businesses in private markets, and they bring community together in service of building the impact investing field. Jessica Droste Yagan, mentioned earlier, is the CEO of Impact Engine.

- **Beyond Capital Ventures** is focused on making investments with deep social impact, with its final close anticipated in 2021. This fund will invest in conscious leaders creating the next wave of innovations addressing basic goods and services in emerging markets. The fund will be aligned with the Sustainable Development Goals and will address macro trends like population growth, distribution of essentials, and technology-enabled solutions.

While these funds are not an official investment recommendation, I know the firms and investment managers personally and have been impressed with their work.

Consider applying your entire investment portfolio to a specific theme or set of themes across different asset classes. In order to impact the environment, you could invest in renewable technology ETFs and the best fossil fuel companies that are attempting to be more sustainable (if you view that as positive progress toward impact). You could also invest in private businesses that are pioneering environmentally friendly technologies in the mobility sector or a sustainable forestry fund. There are multiple ways to integrate an issue you are passionate about with these deeper strategies.

When I look through the top holdings of most ESG funds, I am often surprised that they comprise large technology company stocks and even include The Walt Disney Company, which has a track record of not treating stakeholders equally.[85] While these companies do score well on certain factors, that does not mean their practices and philosophy will resonate with your vision of conscious investing. You may want to seek out more aligned ways to bring your values into your money or start with other areas (time, consumer habits, network, your voice) of your life if the best options available to you are liquid ESG funds.

It is crucial to start *somewhere*. Doing something today that moves toward your goals is better than waiting until tomorrow.

PASSING THE B CORPORATION TEST

In 2007, a new kind of corporation forever changed the business landscape: the B Corporation. This new class of corporation is focused on balancing profit and purpose with a strict set of standards for social and environmental performance, public transparency, and legal accountability. Through these standards, B Corporations hope to accelerate the shift toward a more inclusive and sustainable economy by creating high-quality jobs with dignity and purpose.[86]

Companies interested in becoming a B Corporation must undergo a thorough certification process. The assessment zeros in on company attributes such as environmental impact, workplace diversity, and social impact. Even a company's environmental policy for their remote workers is scrutinized (which has become increasingly important in the post-COVID-19 economy).

The rigorous process can last up to a year. Not all B Corporations have an aligned set of values, but all of them have clearly defined their values. Ben and Jerry's is an example of a B Corporation with a focus on the company's employees. As a corporation, it strives to treat its employees well and create a positive working environment. You can visit the B Corporation website to learn how Ben and Jerry's scored on the overall B Corporation assessment, which is broken down by different areas. The company has a stated goal and purpose, and the score makes transparent how the company is meeting these expectations.

While Ben and Jerry's offers one example, every company interprets and approaches its B Corporation status in its own way. Kickstarter, for instance, focuses on a multitude of stakeholders, including employees, communities, the environment, and its customers. The company's mission is to provide support for underserved or purpose-driven enterprises. Another B Corporation, the chocolate company Alter Eco strongly values environmental impact and strives to make its supply chain fully sustainable. Finally, while some B Corporations sell products or provide services that are fully and obviously aligned with their values, others, like the social media management platform Hootsuite, may not offer a product that immediately reflects their values. However, their efforts within impact areas such as community and workforce consistently score the highest among registered B Corporations.

The B Corporation certification process is rigorous and thorough, down to small details. Increasingly, investors are recognizing B Corporations as a class of company that performs at a standard above that of other businesses—and the next generation of consumers and investors are paying attention to these designations as well. There are other markers of companies that are committed to more than simply the financial bottom line. Some are active adopters of the ESG reporting standards of SASB (the Sustainability Accounting Standards Board). This sends the signal that management is demanding more from their business, which often attracts additional investment and drives value. As such, businesses that care about the E, S, and G attributes of their companies present an opportunity for investment.

As more and more B Corporations become listed on public markets, the B Corporation test can also be effective criteria to screen for investments. There are already private funds being set up to target and invest in B Corporations. And if you apply a scan of B Corporation criteria to other companies, you will likely begin to develop a filter for what matters to you.

WHERE DOES YOUR MONEY SLEEP AT NIGHT?

Jennifer Kenning often asks the question, "Where does your money sleep at night?" The banking system is often overlooked as a source of values and impact—more than any portfolio of investments. It can be the best starting point for investors with little excess investment capital looking to do good. Simply put, when you put your money into a bank account, your money is lent to borrowers that pay the bank interest on a loan. By making thoughtful choices about what you do or do not choose to finance, you help to accelerate important transitions in energy, employment, equality, and social programs. A bank account is very much like an investment in the impact it can have. Every time you deposit your money into a bank, you are creating impact. Consider the possibility that some banks might lend your money to companies with values which do not align with yours. The ideal scenario is that the bank is lending in line with your values—perhaps to your local community or to businesses owned by women or people of color—who are left out of traditional finance. The more you think about the impact your cash in the bank is having, the fuller the picture of the good your money can do.

Let us look at Bank of the West as an example. The bank describes itself as a place to bank your money where it matters, giving you the option to open a checking account with a bank that finances a sustainable tomorrow with your capital.

Another bank, Aspiration, follows the motto *do well, do good*. Aspiration also manages an environmentally focused ETF, the Redwood Fund, and they also offer something called Planet Protection, which automatically makes a day of driving carbon neutral for their banking clients.[87] Aspiration is also certified as a B Corporation. See how you can begin to use B Corporation certifications as a filter for your conscious investing decisions?

According to the Banking on Climate Change report, most well-known banks are the top funders of fossil fuels by a wide margin.[88] Not only is this inconsistent with a focus on climate action, but it is also inconsistent with SDG Goal 10, Reduced Inequalities. As the report correctly notes, the fossil fuel industry has a long history of human rights abuses—especially against indigenous peoples and at-risk communities—a history that has resulted in legal challenges.

This example shows that, when not thinking about all stakeholders, companies can do harm to systems that overlap. In this case, climate change and human rights abuses equate to inequalities intersecting to become a much greater problem. More specifically, intersectional environmentalism is a movement around climate change and how it impacts different communities in different ways. Typically, Black and indigenous people of color, as well as low-income communities and women in developing countries, are impacted disproportionately by climate change. Leah Thomas, founder of Intersectional Environmentalist, a platform named after the movement that advocates for people and planet and stands for inclusivity, helps to advocate for knowledge around intersectionality and relationships between climate and social justice.[89]

Thinking about how the impact of your investments can be intersectional can be powerful in that addressing one issue area can have not only a double bottom line but also a triple bottom line—including people, planet, and profit. If there are multiple areas where the company is producing strong impact, either positive or negative, the investment's overall impact could be amplified. Intersectionality is similar to the concept of systems thinking addressed earlier. Often, one naturally leads to the other. When you think about the whole system in which a specific issue or problem exists, you begin to see how a single problem can create multiple consequences that often go beyond the sector on which you are focusing.

If you care deeply about the environment and the Paris Agreement, which calls for finance flows to be consistent with a pathway toward low greenhouse gas emissions, a traditional bank may not be right for you. Despite the fact that many of these banks claim to support The Paris Agreement, their actions do not yet match this claim. As an optimist and strong believer that pressure from clients, shareholders, and other stakeholders can affect change, I am hopeful to see that J.P. Morgan Chase adopted a Paris-Aligned financing commitment in the fall of 2020. As part of its commitment, J.P. Morgan Chase will establish intermediate emission targets for 2030 for its financing portfolio. The firm will focus on the oil and gas, electric power, and automotive manufacturing sectors and set targets on a sector-by-sector basis.

There are better and more accessible options. Banks that very clearly and publicly state their values and screening practices—local credit unions, Beneficial State Bank, Bank of the West, and Triados Bank in Europe—are a good start for a more conscious banking relationship. There are also a host of B Corporation banks, which are held to an even higher standard. Just like with your investments, ask which bank finances what *you* believe in? Find one that is authentically committed to more than its shareholders and the work they do and that is proud to share their process with other like-minded stakeholders.

As I have become a conscious investor, a holistic commitment to purpose has become as important as where our money is invested. Imagine that you are given the following choices:

1. Having a fully aligned portfolio, but with a bank that is invested in a way that defies your values, or
2. Having a portfolio that will get to where you want one day but that is with a smaller bank that is conscious of its activities and lends to local businesses, communities of color, and female founders.

What would you choose?

OUR FAMILY'S STORY

Over the years, my husband and I have worked hard to make our investment portfolio more consistent with our values. When we were presented with supposedly sustainable funds from our bank, we realized that we needed a more holistic approach than what a private banking relationship could offer. When we were presented with supposedly sustainable fund investment options from our bank, upon due diligence, we realized the options presented did not fit with the depth with which we intended to express our values. As a result, we decided to take a more holistic approach than what a traditional banking relationship could offer.

After a conversation with our wealth manager, we decided to hire an advisor in order to explore ways to deepen our focus on social and environmental impact in our investment portfolio. Knowing that this work is a process, we are constantly reevaluating our choices and making decisions that are in line with our core values.

We have been fortunate to have an advisor we trust to steward our impact goals. In my experience and through my observation, not all advisers have the same training and interests. Generally, unless your advisor has a stated intention to integrate your values into their investment recommendation, you will not be offered what you need, unless your advisor is willing to learn.

Because the traditional banking relationship was not entirely working for us, we found another way to incorporate what we care about into our portfolio. This meant paying slightly more and hiring another person to assist, but the decision was well worth it, giving us the comfort and peace of mind that our portfolio was moving in the right direction, even if it is not fully there yet.

USING ALL YOUR TOOLS

It is possible that some of your philanthropy offers impact investment as a part of its offering to donors. Often this type of investment can be structured as a loan or repayable grant to a nonprofit, but there is increasing innovation to use philanthropy as a means for impact investing. Be thoughtful of how your philanthropy can help catalyze investment that may not be well-tested or yet a proven strategy first, rather than looking to your philanthropy as your only tool for conscious investing. An area in the United States where there has been growing innovation as a vehicle for becoming an impact investor through one's charitable giving is Donor-Advised Funds (DAF). DAFs are increasingly offering impact investment options to their donors. If you have a DAF, it may be an excellent way for you to get started as an impact investor. Groups like CapShift work with DAF holders to structure impact investments, while ImpactAssets offers impact investment options directly to DAF-holders.

frameworks for measuring your impact

In addition to reaching toward goals, such as the SDGs, there are other norms and standards for thinking about the impact your investments are having. The Impact Management Project (IMP) provides investors with a common logic to understand their impact on the planet, so they can "reduce the negative and increase the positive."

In service of that objective, the IMP has identified what are called the five dimensions of impact:

1. **What** tells us what outcomes the enterprise is contributing to and how important the outcomes are to stakeholders.
2. **Who** tells us which stakeholders are experiencing the outcome and how underserved they were prior to the enterprise's effect.
3. **How Much** tells us how many stakeholders experienced the outcome, what degree of change they experienced, and for how long they experienced the outcome.
4. **Contribution** tells us whether an enterprise's and/or investor's efforts resulted in outcomes that were likely better than what would have occurred otherwise.
5. **Risk** tells us the likelihood that the impact will be different than expected.[90]

These five dimensions are based on the consensus opinions and experiences of impact investors who have spent decades measuring their own impact. It is no surprise, then, that they assist in focusing on key areas, but they also offer a useful roadmap for looking at the data.

Another useful way to define and understand what impact data you want to measure comes from the International Finance Corporation (IFC). The IFC's set of eight standards was written specifically with their own investments in mind. However, they are valuable to anyone seeking to more accurately define and measure their impact. These performance standards are risk management, labor resource efficiency, community, land resettlement, biodiversity, indigenous people, and cultural heritage.[91] More specifically in the area of labor resource efficiency, the IFC explains that "for any business, their workforce is their most valuable asset. A sound worker/manager relationship is key to the success of any enterprise."[92]

The IFC also has a strict set of operating principles for funds. To dive deep into how a well-established investor recommends that funds measure their impact, you can research the IFC's *Operating Principles for Impact Management*, which provides some excellent in-depth research. However, if you are investing in funds, it is useful to determine whether these funds have signed on to the Operating Principles for Impact Management. These principles provide guidance for thinking about impact, defining impact objectives across the portfolio, considering the potentially negative impacts of each investment, and understanding the sustained impact of your investment when exiting.[93]

In 2020, the big four accounting firms, in cooperation with the World Economic Forum, released an ESG reporting framework designed to measure stakeholder capitalism. This simple framework outlines four areas—principles of governance, planet, people, and prosperity—that give focus to the key markers of stakeholder capitalism. Because large companies are often the clients of these big four accounting companies, this framework stands a good chance of being integrated into how companies express their own ESG-related activities.[94]

As you can see, there is no single standard or framework from which to consider the impact of your investments. However, the IMP, the IFC, and the framework put out by the big four accounting firms and the World Economic Forum offer internationally recognized guidance to help investors think about their investment decisions.

CONSCIOUS INVESTING STRATEGIES

- Avoid a company that has positive intentions but is not financially sustainable (unless your investment strategy is to invest in an area with concessionary returns for a specific reason).
- Impact investments are investments in the people behind the companies that match your values, often conscious leaders.
- Consider coinvesting with others to share resources and learn.
- Remain active and engaged when possible. This will help you fulfill your purpose and see your investments thrive.

DO YOUR DUE DILIGENCE

Due diligence is no more than getting to know the deep details of what you are investing in, whether the investment matches with your initial plan and intentions and verifies the possibility of how you expect that investment to perform—in other words, how much money and impact you intend to make and how much risk is involved in the investment. Due diligence does not have to involve all numbers and should not be a mere checklist. Rather, it is a defined step-by-step process that allows investors to holistically become experts on both their investments and the people behind them.

During the due diligence process, from sourcing an investment to understanding how to exactly invest your capital, facts are verified, and risks are quantified. For example, if a company has a major competitor selling a product that already has significant market traction, that detail will be taken into account in the due diligence process and the ultimate investment decision.

To understand why due diligence is important, consider how you make purchase decisions in other scenarios. Would you buy a car without test driving it? This is the same mindset you should take when approaching your investments.

Not only is due diligence important, the specific process by which investors learn more about an investment opportunity has its own value. A due diligence process can start informally. After identifying a potential investment from a set of opportunities, a due diligence process may start with one to two introductory conversations between the investor and, in the case of Beyond Capital's investment scope, the company's founder. These conversations establish whether there is a mutual fit and interest, and the tone can serve as the foundation for a longer-term relationship. This scenario may be different if you are evaluating a fund, or individual stock or security.

After initial conversations have allowed the investor and investee to better gauge fit, the due diligence process moves into more formal stages. In the example of direct investing, it can be important for investors to stage questions through the formal due diligence process. The due diligence process is also designed to help entrepreneurs to be disciplined and think through their ideas and business models. However, each question from an investor requires work from a company and, ultimately, time away from running the business, which is something to be aware of when you are evaluating an investment opportunity. While this level of detail in due diligence applies mostly to direct investments only, you can draw inspiration from these practices to inform how you analyze other types of companies as well. Overall, due diligence has a ripple effect on the readiness of the business to attract additional professional and institutional capital to future funding rounds.

At Beyond Capital, we employ a six-stage process from sourcing and screening potential investments through more detailed levels of review, including background checks on management team members, reference calls with customers, and a deep dive into the company's financial model. Our team meets every week to discuss potential investment opportunities and eventually recommends investments to the investment committee and board. Regular check-ins with your portfolio performance or advisors are important to continue to move the process along.

Impact investors need to consider additional elements and ask questions about the fidelity to social and environmental goals in the due diligence process. In my view, conscious investors have an even higher duty to conduct a comprehensive investigation of a company. That is because there is a social or environmental impact at stake. When an entrepreneur builds a company to solve for good, it is the investor's responsibility to peel back the layers to ensure its foundation is strong and has a viable impact potential.

Overall, any opportunity screened as an impact investment would have to meet double- or triple-bottom-line investment goals.

When performing due diligence, a conscious investor might ask the following questions:

1. What is the social and/or environmental impact the investment is targeting?
2. Is the investment committed to serve a population/goal you care about?
3. Is the core product or service deemed a necessity by the stakeholders the investment is serving?
4. How does the investment monitor and evaluate the performance of its impact activities? What are the implied results of those metrics?
5. Is the impact a paradigm shift or a fundamental change in the approach or underlying assumptions?
6. Is the investment committed to sustainability and market-based solutions?
7. Is the team committed to measure social and/or environmental impact in a holistic and systematic manner?
8. Are there other tangential benefits to society or the environment of this investment?
9. Does the investment have any relevant impact affiliations (e.g., B Corporation status)?

There is always more information to uncover in a due diligence process. As such, it is important for investors to identify and focus on which information is crucial to an investment decision. Ultimately, an effective investment decision may be made on just a few key data points uncovered in diligence. And either way, investors aim to ensure the success of the investment with their post-investment portfolio management efforts.

At Beyond Capital, some direct investments—from initial consideration to investment—have taken six months, others only a few. With that said, given the depth of information requested and provided, a generosity of time is often necessary to result in a beneficial and impactful investment decision. When it comes to public-market or fund investing, you may be able to make a decision much quicker, especially if your values are defined up front.

Still, thorough due diligence can be a lengthy process. But the rewards often beget more rewards. I have found due diligence unlocks a well of learning and ideas, for both the entrepreneur and investor. Due diligence can lead to lower risk later on in the investment process, including structural risk to a nascent company's capitalization table and its early-stage investors. It can also ensure a strong, sustainable relationship between investor and investee, one established on transparency, trust, and respect. These elements go a long way for anyone collaborating on a shared mission to better the world.

As you ask critical questions, there are resources that help illuminate groups that are systemically exclusionary or systemically racist. The "Racial Justice Exclusion List" provided by the social justice investing firm Robasciotti and Philipson is one of them, but it is not alone.[95] As you research, think of these as resources but not the final word on the conversation. And as always, let your own values guide your decisions.

MATHILDE'S STORY

I work with an amazing woman named Mathilde, who is part of Generation Z and is very passionate about integrating her social values into her life. In her eyes, her job, career, and savings should be aligned with her core beliefs as a matter of fact, not as a paradigm shift. Mathilde has always talked about investing her life savings in a more sustainable way, and she has inspired me to do more since she joined my team at Beyond Capital.

Mathilde recognized that due diligence is also about asking questions. And, in order to reach her goal of a sustainable retirement savings, she sought out more. When she first set up her retirement savings, investing sustainably was not advertised as an option. But when she began asking questions, she realized that she could invest her retirement savings in ESG-screened funds. That one possibility gave Mathilde's life so much more meaning and purpose than she had before. She felt empowered to realign her values and invest where it could do some good.

The reality is that meaningful investment strategies are rarely made widely available, especially if your investments are made through large brokerage houses. If enough people like Mathilde feel brave enough to ask the right questions, these opportunities might become more common. In general, due diligence can be applied to all areas of aligning our money and our values, including asking more of our retirement and savings.

When Wall Street veteran Sallie Krawcheck set up an investing organization called Ellevest in 2014, with a built-in conscious investing option that you can switch on or off as you set up the account, investing literally could not have been made any easier for Mathilde. She chose to invest her savings in Ellevest and has been happy with her portfolio's purpose ever since.

best practices

Now that you understand a little more about the full extent of impact investing, here are some best practices that you can deploy. While some of these recommendations apply more specifically to direct impact investing, others apply to any and all impact investing and conscious use of resources. Informed decisions will yield results. Many cannot make every decision alone, but resources and professional guidance are available to help.

INVEST IN PEOPLE

With any investment, you are not just investing in a business plan or idea or even solely a fully formed business. You are always investing in the founders behind the company. It is important, then, that those leaders' values match your own.

One example of how investing in a company rather than in people could go wrong is the company WeWork, which had a tremendous vision of creating a community around workplaces—bringing professionals together, distributing their work, and allowing them more flexibility in their lives. This vision apparently resonated with investors, who poured more VC money into WeWork than the total combined amount of funding received by female founders in 2019![96] Unfortunately, the WeWork CEO, Adam Neumann, turned out to be an unreliable steward of that vision, and the company suffered as a result. Not only was his lacking leadership a disappointment to the mission, it was a risk to the entire business. Investors soon realized that Neumann's lacking moral leadership could impact financial return. Once again, social, environmental, and governance factors are increasingly being seen as risk factors for investment.

Granted, this is a very public example of what can go wrong when investors focus only on a business model over the leadership behind it. In most cases, investors are close enough to their investment to know exactly who they are investing in directly, though they will still have plenty of resources for making informed decisions.

You can still get a good sense of the values the company or fund leadership instilled in the organization that they have created. Verifiable sources exist to shed light on how companies treat their employees or how they engage with their local community. When you see how they treat stakeholders, you will know the kind of impact they will make.

For example, my cohost on *The Beyond Capital Podcast*, Ed Stevens, is the CEO of a company called Preciate, which focuses on building relational wealth within purpose-driven companies by focusing on strong and authentic relationships. The mission of the company is to bring the power of togetherness technology to every company on the planet—and Preciate may just do it.

Preciate's business model shows how companies build strong relationships. Not only do employees receive recognition on their company account, but the recognition that they receive also is saved and kept with the employee, giving them a profile that can be taken from job to job. By creating employee profiles, these companies are showing that they care about building stronger relationships in their workplaces, treating their employees well, and providing relational wealth in addition to their salaries, bonuses, and benefits. Through these efforts, Preciate is creating a social currency and putting value not only on relational wealth but also on how that wealth can be built up over time, which can help investors make better decisions about the health of a company.

IT MIGHT LOOK GOOD ON PAPER

Sometimes, an investment that looks good at first turns out not to be the most logical or the most values-aligned investment. For instance, a wealth manager offers you the opportunity to invest in a portfolio that they think meets your goals for integrating your values into your investments. They tell you that this *is* an impact investment with a major financial opportunity because the global economy is changing and companies are adjusting their business practices to seize new opportunities and manage risk.

Your first reaction is enthusiastic—here is a chance to become an impact investor with less administrative cost and a promise of financial return no different than what you are used to. Then, you look deeper into the details of the fund, and you realize the impact strategy could be better thought through and more differentiated from other investment options. The fund may also not be investing in the sectors you are passionate about. Or it may not be active enough in influencing companies to do their part with voting proxies. Just because a well-known financial institution or wealth manager has recommended an "impact investing" fund for your portfolio does not mean that it meets your specific goals.

If you have invested in a fund with this profile, do not beat yourself up—even if you have already invested. Success is a process. By simply becoming aware of areas to pay closer attention to in your due diligence, you have taken great strides forward. Thinking about stakeholders and the larger system in which a fund or company operates can often illuminate how a business or investment strategy may not be exactly in line with your desired impact. Making an investment that *does* meet some of your impact goals is better than not investing at all.

AVOID THE MISSION TRAP

You will learn about a lot of investment opportunities that sound promising, innovative, incredibly impactful, and sometimes too good to be true. Someone will tell you about a magical company solving a big social problem, and its founders are well-intentioned and working hard. But after looking under the hood, it might not appear to be a sustainable business that can grow and scale lasting financial and social performance.

For instance, at Beyond Capital, when we think a company is over-promising, we review their financial projections and find that there could be more rigor involved in setting forth the business expansion strategy or that there is some naivete in how they are achieving their goals that will create barriers to growth in the future.

While additional investigation is needed, this company's promise may be too good to be true—and it should probably be avoided if your plans for your own investments are to produce sustainable and viable financial and social returns. There are, however, times where pioneering a technology may require more risk. But in general, when looking for balance of financial and social returns, avoiding skewed or unsustainable impact is advisable.

Some simple common questions to ask are how does the business make money? Does the company's business model add up to a sustainable and profitable business? Are its activities extracting or creating value for the stakeholders?

Remember that you are not only investing in a company's mission. You are investing in the visionaries, contributors, and role players behind the mission and the stakeholders affected by it. If the team has not given serious thought to how their business is going to operate—or how they are going to make money—then it is time to invest your money elsewhere. Impact investing is investing for financial, social, environmental, and technological return. While there is some personal proclivity and nuance in the exact balance, it is ultimately important to consider each aspect of what you are looking to achieve.

IMPACT WASHING

Similar to the mission trap is the phenomenon of impact washing and greenwashing in impact investing. This is why it is crucial to implement your values directly, rather than converting your resources to generically categorized impact investments and feeling good about it. Clear values create a compass that can guide your decisions and set a benchmark for measuring success.

My colleague and friend, Matt Raimondi, is the Beyond Capital Director of Social Impact. He is also an Associate Director at Sustainalytics, which is a leading independent ESG and corporate governance research, ratings, and analytics firm that tracks twelve thousand global companies in emerging markets and developed markets. When I asked him about companies self-reporting ESG data, he explained that the nature of most ESG ratings is that they rely on company disclosure and publicly available data. This can lead to scoring bias for companies with more robust reporting and is something Sustainalytics tries to account for in their methodology. And because ESG ratings are based on company self-reporting, it is difficult to know the truth and where impact washing has taken over.

For example, Matt explained that while Sustainalytics rates oil and gas one of the highest-risk industries, many companies in this sector put significant resources into their sustainability reports and marketing—even though, in reality, those efforts are often a very small part of their business. At the same time, many of these companies are involved in environmental controversies. For example, Exxon made a bold claim that they were reducing greenhouse gas emissions to attract attention and gain ESG status, when in reality, this was a very small part of their business.[97] The key is to ask questions that get to the heart of the impact the company is having.

Raimondi also highlighted that self-reported ESG disclosures vary widely from company to company, both in content and in quality. Furthermore, the result is that an ETF portfolio can end up becoming overconcentrated with companies that report more information than smaller businesses. This can be problematic for a few reasons. First, if the ETF seeks to track a benchmark (such as a market index), it might not be able to fully represent that by excluding businesses that lack ESG data and reporting. Second, reporting also varies by region, with developed market companies tending to have more robust disclosure and reporting on ESG.

Raimondi believes that in order to have a meaningful understanding of what a company's ESG disclosure reporting actually means would require a standard reporting framework. One of these frameworks, SASB, is making strides in providing a standard reporting framework for companies, but it is still not widely adopted or required by law.[98] Raimondi's company, Sustainalytics, offers another potential solution, since the company can provide a more consistent and comparable assessment across a broad universe of companies that they cover.[99] Most likely, a top-tier advisor or fund manager will consult with a firm like Sustainalytics on the ratings for their investment recommendations.

Still, you should be informed, and there are plenty of companies out there that do not engage in impact washing. Many of these businesses may have good intentions but lack rigor in their approach. However, other firms may be acting out of opportunism with impact investing on the rise. If a company appears to overlook certain activities, if they intentionally conceal damaging information, or if you find it difficult to construct an accurate picture of how they operate, then it is likely not a good investment opportunity. Here are some warning signs to consider with each investment:

False Reporting

ESG research begins with bottom-up, company-specific data, much of which is voluntarily disclosed by the companies themselves. A company looking to exaggerate its impact could easily complete false or misleading reports.

Lies through Omission

A company could claim that their product or service is good for the environment. And in one way, it might very well be. But producing that product could also come with unintended consequences that impact the environment in other negative ways. An example is the rare earth metals that power mobile phones. Mining these metals are toxic to the environment and harmful to the health of individuals involved in extracting them. Examples like this illustrate the importance of thinking through the big picture whenever possible.

Imagery and Misleading Statements

Some companies utilize imagery and make misleading statements that entice investors and consumers that could be clues to potential greenwashing. These include overuse of environmental imagery or misleading labels using terms like "natural" or "environmentally friendly" without further explanation of methodology or lack of a legitimate certification like Fair Trade to back up these claims.

Other forms of greenwashing could include overselling a particular ESG quality of a business while ignoring another—in other words, incorporating hidden tradeoffs. For example, the electric car industry may show promise and tout the positive benefits of fossil-fuel-free transportation, but there remains an open discussion on the environmental impact of producing the lithium-ion batteries used to power them.

If you plan to be extremely intentional with one particular sector or area focus, understand that some impact investing opportunities do employ a "lesser of two evils strategy." For example, "greener" fuel companies happily promote their use of hydrogen as a clean fuel source, even if their overall practices are not sustainable. Once again, to identify these forms of greenwashing, it is important to do your own due diligence or hire a trusted advisor. Overall, companies may score well on ESG rankings, but it is important to understand what they are assessing and look beyond their marketing or rhetoric to understand what is driving the score.

BE ACTIVE WITH YOUR PORTFOLIO

Check in with your portfolio on a regular basis, at least monthly, but sometimes daily or weekly (although I tend to prefer the long-term investment approach). This is a good practice for any investor. If you are investing in companies directly, find ways to help businesses achieve their impact goals.

Active screening gives way to active impact measurement. Because companies are self-reporting their data, try to request as much transparency in reporting frameworks as possible.

Taking a more active approach, you can be more open to selecting companies based on their core values and the ways in which they align with yours. For example, when sourcing Beyond Capital's investment in Numida, a financial lending business for small- and medium-sized companies in Uganda, our initial review of the business was based on the social impact we wanted to achieve on enterprise development in East Africa. Small- and medium-sized businesses create jobs at twice the pace of large corporations. Social enterprises are also filling gaps in critical goods and service provision. And yet, 86 percent of social enterprises in emerging markets say access to financial backing is a major constraint. We were looking for the investment opportunity to help entrepreneurs scale and invest in a business that would generate financial return in our portfolio.

Say your goal is to invest in companies with diverse management teams or those that have some racial diversity on the board of directors. In theory, by investing in such companies (or funds that take this approach), you are actively supporting that movement. In reality, this is an example of a more passive, diluted approach to investment. This is why I advocate that you find ways, if possible, to think beyond superficial screens. Rather than checking a box on a report, you can decide to support companies with solutions to complex problems or decide not to invest in companies that lack governance by underrepresented groups. To become more active, you can invest directly in people of color, for example, who have founded and run their own companies, that possess true equal representation on the company's board, and take an unbiased approach to diversity. Passive strategies often equal avoidance—for example, you are avoiding companies that invest in tobacco, firearms, the dirtiest fossil fuels, or animal cruelty. Active strategies apply positive screens for the good your money can do. You can actively seek out companies with sustainability in their culture and pinpoint those that market their products responsibly and demonstrate the best practices in governance—like Left Coast Naturals, Avangard Innovative, Revolution Foods, the thousands of B Corporations, or other purpose-driven companies in your community. You can find companies which display diversity in age, gender, religion, race, disability, and sexual orientation. You can focus on companies which meet human rights standards and do not just commit to meeting standards with lacking action. An active approach is to find a company that bakes a rejection of human rights abuses into their culture. Parker Clay is a leather goods B Corporation, which employs mostly women, many of whom were formerly in prostitution. The women earn a sustainable livelihood, a type of employment that most have never had. Parker Clay's key values are ingrained in the company culture; with every purchase customers receive an explanation of the business and reporting on the impact progress the business has had. As a shareholder, that information likely would be reported back to you, so you could measure the impact of your investment as well.

THE DIVESTINVEST MOVEMENT

In order for your investments to be successful in the ways you envision, you will need to have the right practices in place to set your values into action. That is the focus of the DivestInvest movement, a strategy designed to accelerate our transition to sustainable energy.

DivestInvest came about when a group of impact investors and philanthropists who cared about the environment realized they were funding fossil fuels in their investment portfolios. Since doing so was antithetical to their goals, they decided to take a two-pronged approach: divesting from fossil fuels and instead investing in climate solutions. This movement has now spanned all areas of investment—university endowment, healthcare institutions, governments, individuals, NGOs, pension funds, trusts and foundations, private companies, and family offices.

The DivestInvest movement is a positive example of how you can look deeper into your portfolio and discover areas that directly contradict your values. Divesting from those investments is a good start, but going the extra step and investing in the solution creates a much more positive net benefit.[100]

Taking this approach one step further, divesting from businesses that are antithetical to your values can deprive companies of money indirectly by increasing their cost of equity, which is the return shareholders expect if they are to be enticed to buy or hold the company's stocks. And a higher cost of equity can lead to a company raising less money from share sales. Because some businesses do not need to raise additional funding on the stock market, if you own a stock you do not agree with, a better way to influence the company would be to engage at shareholder meetings, file complaints with regulators, or issue statements to the news media.

DEVELOP A DIVERSIFIED PORTFOLIO

As a general investing principle, a diversified portfolio over multiple assets carries less risk. A diverse portfolio also allows for a cross section of impact, even within specific themes. For example, if SDG Goal 13, Climate Action, is an area you want to mobilize your resources in favor of, you can target environmental impact across multiple areas of your portfolio, addressing your area of focus more holistically.

Remember that impact investing is a mindset. What I mean is that impact investing is a reframing of how our money can be utilized to express our desires and intentions for a better society. It is a paradigm shift that you can practically tap into over time to make your investments and money a more integrated part of your life.

CHAPTER 8

find a like-minded
community

My early career was spent working in hedge funds, influenced by the extravagance of money and what it could buy. In that environment, the underlying, unspoken goal is often to show off what you have to those around you. Even if my aim was not to boast, I learned very well to lead with wealth and then, in my early twenties, grew to dislike that about myself. Once in a conversation with Brian Axelrad, whom I mentioned earlier, he shared that his work at Beyond Capital was the reason that he was thriving in his career. I realized I could relate—the work I do every day and the progress I have made are interwoven into my identity and its language. Early on, that meant leading with money. Now, circumstances have changed. After a while, talking about restaurants, hotels, travel, even companies (lacking purpose) to invest in, and sometimes even the musings of the glamorous art community (although art still brings me immense joy) felt less interesting. I already mentioned that I do not believe in "selling it all" and escaping from money altogether. My goal is to set personal standards for my life that feel right, where my family and I can thrive and contribute responsibly.

It has taken time, effort, and a different sort of community to reach where I am today, but I do not feel like I have to compete anymore. I would not be who I am without Beyond Capital, the people I work with, the conversations my work has inspired, and the community it has introduced me to.

In his talks, positive psychology expert Shawn Achor outlines a specific study that measured people's perception of hiking a hill. The study concluded that hikers *overestimate* the time and effort it takes to hike a hill if they are doing it alone, but they *underestimate* the time and effort it takes to climb if they are hiking in a group. There is a scientific element to the human desire to achieve in groups—living out your values on your own is going to be far lonelier than if you found a community to be part of.

This is especially important for conscious investing. While I have watched plenty of people attempt to become conscious investors on their own, I have also found that the experience is much less rewarding and effective than learning from others. It does not feel like work when you are all in it together. The hill does not seem so steep.

Like Achor's analogy, conscious investing takes time and effort—and doing it right will likely take longer than you expect. But research has shown that diverse viewpoints yield stronger decisions and results. In a 2015 McKinsey report, for instance, researchers examined 366 public companies. Those that were in the top 25 percent in terms of racial and ethnic diversity were 25 percent more likely to generate financial returns above the industry mean. Meanwhile, companies in the top 25 percent for gender diversity were 15 percent more likely to perform above the industry mean.[101] And any task shared within a group, even the most difficult task, yields greater results. In the process, you learn from others and become a more effective investor.

It is also important to join and be inspired by communities that may be pursuing impact differently to learn another approach. For example, Goop has emerged as a source of information and conversations that I would not have otherwise found. Whether the topic is health, elevating women and people of color, or anti-inflammatory foods, I have regularly learned something new over the years. I also have been inspired by the tone of the Goop content. Through Goop, I met Stacey Lindsay, the Editorial Director of *The Conscious Investor* online magazine, where each week we shed light on the nuanced conversations around impact investing. The aim is to speak to a wider audience and use journalism as a means to shed light on individuals, businesses, and communities committed to doing good.

Throughout the years, the Toniic community has continually pushed me to challenge my own beliefs, practices, and assumptions about my personal impact, my role in social change, and how I can be a servant leader. This community brings to life Margaret Mead's famous saying, "Never doubt that a small group of thoughtful, committed citizens can change the world."

engaging with your community

Independent of impact investing, there still remains doubt and fear of judgment around money that discourages many from realizing their potential to do good. Even if you might feel like you have overcome a taboo, and even if you have the best intentions, you might worry that others will try to poke holes in your values, in your strategy, and in your everyday behavior. Do not let these fears stop you from finding a community that can support and add value to your work.

Leading a life of purpose can be a vulnerable experience. At this point, I am comfortable with the values I aim to live by, but like everyone else, sometimes I still question my purpose and actions. Am I intentional enough? Can I always do better (read: perfectionism)? Do I always strive to deepen my impact in all areas of my life? Yes, on all counts. That said, I am only human. My life has a carbon footprint, and I know it. But that does not stop me from seeking out and connecting with others in communities centered on doing good and investing with their values.

The Toniic community has helped me explore the extent to which I want to have an impact with my money and resources. It has helped me to find my equilibrium, the place where I am comfortable with my personal impact. However, I did not always find that balance by interacting with conscious investors who agreed with me. Rather, I have learned from those who have occasionally politely challenged my opinions. This network of conscious investors has made me aware of different combinations of wealth and impact, constantly encouraging me to challenge my own beliefs, practices, and assumptions.

You do not have to be an advanced impact investor to strive for meaning and purpose in community, and certain groups may not fit your needs. In the case of Toniic, in addition to paying an annual membership fee, members must be accredited investors. The goal should simply be to find and engage a community of like-minded individuals who you can share with and learn from.

If you are part of an industry networking group, you may find a subset of members who are interested in taking action with their money. For instance, I am involved in the 100 Women in Finance network. While not related to impact investing specifically, this community of fifteen thousand women—all focused on helping each other reach their professional potential at each career stage—has been invaluable as a source of connection.

A few starting points to join or build a community:

- **Community foundations.** Popping up all over the country, community foundations serve as beachheads for community giving. The Community Foundation of Dallas, for instance, galvanizes giving in the community through annual events such as the North Texas Giving Day, which raised $59 million in 2020. Most of these community foundations offer investing options focused on impact investing and are a great starting point for those interested in joining a community rather than starting their own.

- **Beyond Capital Ambassador Program and Acumen Partners.** Both Beyond Capital and Acumen Fund, another organization focused on impact investing in later stages, have designed programs focused on bringing people together around their efforts.[102]

- **Social Venture Partners.** SVP's membership groups may also provide a gateway to communities focused on impact investing. SVP connects donors with mentor engagements with nonprofits in chapters around the United States. But while groups like Social Venture Partners do admirable work, most of their chapters focus on charitable giving rather than impact investing. They are just as focused on doing good, but the philosophy is not exactly the same.

Everyone deserves access to more than philanthropy and ESG negative screening. This stands true even if you are not invested in a specific fund or have a high net worth. There is a tremendous opportunity for communities to form for interested impact investors that would benefit from having a community of like-minded individuals to work with. If racial equality is a core area of focus for you, the Black Lives Matter movement may serve as a starting point for this conversation. If you have not found a community to meet your needs, then consider starting your own.

Find a group of friends, colleagues, and family members who are passionate about the good their money can do. Start meeting with them and talking to them about issues related to what you have learned, the barriers you have encountered, and the different strategies you use. Impact investing is a big umbrella with lots of different focus areas within it, and it can be hard to narrow down one focus area. It is okay if the others in your group do not share exactly the same focus as you. Especially in the early days, the most important thing is to identify and interact with others who are working toward a shared cause.

At Beyond Capital, we like to fund simple solutions to complex problems. Sometimes, the best solutions are the small local ones that can have a wide-reaching impact.

risk and opportunity

Increasingly, institutions and powerful social and environmental forces are changing the world. The largest growing sector of mutual funds is ESG. Half of global consumers would happily pay a premium for a more sustainable product,[103] and by the year 2050, solar and wind are expected to power half the globe.[104] This is useful information, demonstrating investing in the good economy is actually a sounder investment strategy than investing in our current dominant economic model. According to *The Harvard Business Review*, 85 percent of purpose-driven companies show positive top-line growth, whereas that figure drops to 58 percent for companies that are not purpose-driven.[105]

Now is the time to rally around this opportunity—and the best way forward is together. Everyone likes to win, especially in groups. In this moment in time, our community is global and growing. There is absolutely no reason to become conscious of this alone.

Because becoming a conscious investor is about more than just money—it is about finding purpose in your life—having a network of like-minded peers is vital. It could be a group of friends who are aligned in thinking or a more formal group that supports a specific cause or idea. Not only will this community help you have a greater impact, but it will fuel a better life. If you are surrounded by those who are compassionate, empathetic, and contributing beyond themselves, you feel a new sense of motivation to move forward toward purpose and fulfillment.

My executive coach, Keren Eldad, often talks about the value of a "high-vibe tribe" in achieving your goals. Surrounding yourself with others who are working toward your mission is also a feature of The CEO Mindset. When conscious investing, identifying and being part of a community is *just as relevant* as setting goals and aligning your money with your values. Trust me, it will be worth it.

establishing a safe space

After growing up in a family that did not talk much about the specifics of money and investing (social justice *was* a common theme at the dinner table), then entering the workforce as a woman in a sector that historically has not included women in dialogue about money, I found the concept of engaging with others around finances somewhat strange and new at first. But in 2016, after sitting next to an impact investor at a small conference in Garrison, New York, I realized just how important this engagement could be.

His name was Eric, and mid-conversation, he turned to me and asked, "Where is your wealth from?"

In all of the gatherings I have attended, nobody had ever asked me that question directly before. No one had wanted to talk so simply and specifically about money. And yet, it is so critical.

Typically, if you know your friend has capital at their disposal, you assume that they work hard, save up, have sold a business, or inherited their wealth, and that is it. You do not talk about the details much with them. It is true that my husband and I work hard and have done well professionally from a financial standpoint, and that the money from those successes goes toward our investment portfolio. But that moment felt like the first time somebody had acknowledged me as a *person* in the community of impact investors. As soon as someone else knew the origin of the resources (hard work) I intended to use consciously, I felt like part of the impact investing community in a deeper way than ever before.

If I am at a lively dinner party and someone asks me what I do, even if I trust that person, chances are they may never really be able to get to the heart of my work. By asking me such a direct question, Eric was honoring the safe space in which we found ourselves. That level of community, where those involved are encouraged to show up wholeheartedly, is not accessible everywhere, and we both knew that.

The Toniic community is where I began thinking about conscious investing in a holistic way. It is where I realized it could impact all areas of my life because all areas of my life contributed to my personal mission and vision of impact.

Conversations around conscious investing work best in a group setting if everyone fully brings themselves into the conversation. Without allowing for authenticity, conscious investors cannot access their values and beliefs or find purpose in their money. Unlike galas and fancy philanthropic events, this is not about meeting someone else's vision. And it is certainly *not* about buying a $2,000 dress just to sit at a table and listen to people accept awards. (Yes, the charity gala model raises money for a cause. But more money could be raised without the extravagant event taking place—and impact investors care about doing *more* with all resources at their disposal.)

At a conscious investing community gathering, your most authentic self might like to wear makeup and maybe drive your Bentley. Or maybe it is showing up in jeans and a T-shirt. When everyone is there for impact and to support each other, it will not matter. Members of the community can show up as themselves, confident that they are on the same level as everyone around them. There is a lot of joy in showing up with a profound level of authenticity.

There is no movement without community. In order to affect social change that goes beyond money, people must be rallied to a cause. Organizations like Every Town for Gun Safety and Moms Demand Action offer two compelling examples of the power of community. Even though they are virtual communities, they have helped to spark a national movement around gun control in the United States.

RULES AND BOUNDARIES

The boundaries of a community are what keep it safe and comfortable for its members, especially for a topic this potentially vulnerable. Knowing what the rules are, group members feel more comfortable showing up, bringing their social concerns to the table, and being the fullest versions of themselves.

If you want to create your own community, make sure you are doing it for the right reasons, then keep those reasons centered throughout. Be authentic, and allow others to do the same.

I have hosted dozens of Jeffersonian Conversations and Women's gatherings every year, designed precisely to create a space that is safe and comfortable for my network to connect. The goal is to create meaningful gatherings where participants feel they can share. I was recently invited to a small group virtual session with five other women raising venture funds hosted by a women's venture fund law firm. The goal was to support one another in our capital-raising efforts and connect with other female general partners. Because the host created a safe space, each woman in the group shared deeply, often offering top tips on fundraising and ways she has been successful. It was memorable and impactful.

If you are hoping to establish a community of your own, here are some important factors to think about:

1. **Be discreet.** For people to be open about their questions and concerns, they need to know that their discussions will not become public information. Put in place a rigid framework

with consequences if trust is broken, including confidentiality agreements, if desired.

2. **Respect others.** There will be other voices and values in the room. Demonstrate mutual respect for one another, even when your values are different.

3. **Commit to learning.** Becoming a conscious investor is inherently linked to the process of learning, a process that begins with a personal commitment and then radiates outward.

4. **Help your fellow community members.** The more you help others, the more good will come your way.

5. **Prioritize the vision.** If you make an impact investment together, break up the due diligence work, and be oriented toward the success of that investment as a group.

Once you agree on the rules for your community, put an agreement in place so every participant knows what is expected from them and others. Community is a participatory function, where everyone needs to contribute in order to make it work.

RESOURCES FOR GETTING STARTED

BOOKS

- *The Life You Can Save* by Peter Singer
- *The Power of Impact Investing* by Judith Rodin and Margo Brandenburg
- *Manifesto for a Moral Revolution* by Jacqueline Novogratz
- *Real Impact* by Morgan Simon
- *The Purpose of Capital* by Jed Emerson

PUBLICATIONS

- ImpactAlpha
- Bloomberg Green
- *B the Change* (a blog about B Corporations)
- *The Conscious Investor* online magazine
- *The Conscious Investor* Resource Guide for Beginning Impact Investors[106]

PRACTITIONER GROUPS AND COMMUNITIES

- Toniic, *toniic.com*
- Unreasonable Collective, *unreasonablegroup.com/ collective/*
- Invest for Better, *investforbetter.org*
- The Global Impact Investing Network, *thegiin.org*
- Impact investing groups on *meetup.com*

THINK OUTSIDE THE BOX

If you are brand new to impact investing, the best way to know whether something is right for you is to try it. Make an investment. Take part in a gathering and ask yourself if it feels right to be there. Let the first step help inform the next step, then the next.

If you are struggling to identify a community close to you, look to unconventional sources. Is there an opportunity to create a community within your workplace? For the past decade, leaders have shared with me that employees are looking for more than salary from their companies. They are looking to feel engaged and aligned with the work they are doing. Not only does this foster relational wealth and social capital, but it also helps to foster a more positive company culture and improve workplace well-being. Employees want to feel happy. They want community.

The communities around conscious investing are still growing. For now, no group is too small or too atypical. While larger groups will offer more resources and chances for knowledge sharing, a small group of people learning together can be useful and powerful in its own way—and sometimes more action-oriented. Shared purpose creates a huge amount of value for small groups, large networks, and supportive workplaces.

discord happens

By this stage in the conscious investing process, you will have spent a lot of time examining and defining your values. Your values are *yours*, which means there is potential for them to clash with others' values. So, what happens if somebody in your community does not agree with your values or impact?

The values found within my community run the full spectrum. For example, some believe that if you fly on airplanes, then you are doing harm to the environment—period. But in order to do the work that I do, I often fly across the globe quite regularly to cultivate the relationships that aid in having a greater impact consistent with my goals.

I acknowledge that flying has a negative environmental impact, but traveling is part of the overall mission and values that guide me, including social justice, learning from leaders at the top of their game, growing personal wealth in all dimensions and equanimity, and pursuing longevity. I make an effort to be as responsible as I can.

By immersing myself in the conversation in a safe space and being exposed to a range of viewpoints, I am able to find my own moral compass and understand where I want to focus my overall impact. My perspectives may change over time as I continue to grow and refine my personal impact strategy in the next five, ten, or twenty years. But to get there, I first need to understand where I am. In other words, do not be discouraged if somebody disagrees with your own view of impact. As long as you believe in your values enough to want to see that impact through and achieve social and environmental progress, you are taking a step in the right direction.

Be prepared for your values to differ from others', even within a community with a shared desire to make an impact. *You* have to be all in. *You* have to be secure in *your* goals. As long as you know what you are trying to do, you can keep working toward doing the best you possibly can.

Disagreement provides plenty of learning opportunities, making it one of the benefits of a tightly protected community. Look for those opportunities. Learn from those around you, and pay special attention to moments where you are uncomfortable with their choices. Thinking back to the theory of selling everything to become an impact investor—that does not have to be you. While some of my colleagues in the industry do believe that is important, initially, I felt uncomfortable to think in this way. However, in understanding that my approach could be different than theirs, I arrived at a better position for myself.

bringing humanity back into investing

When I asked Jennifer Kenning about the biggest challenges she faces in the industry, she predicted that the traditional financial services industry might try to stop the growth of impact investing. To do this, financial firms that do not consider more than financial goals could provide surface-level investing options to sway their clients or expand into new markets—it would look like their firm was offering impact as a solution, but in reality, that impact would be minimal to nonexistent. Her caution as an investor is against impact washing and greenwashing.

Kenning argues that financial advisors need to become more educated on deeper areas of impact, and that fees should be in line with traditional investment products to avoid cost competition. For conscious investing to become an investable opportunity for a larger group, misleading marketing and greenwashing needs to be eradicated. Only then will we return to our roots of community lending on a large scale, especially to small businesses.

Even so, she believes that conscious investing will become part of the mainstream within the next decade, and a community is an opportunity to grow together, learn from each other, and help the industry become more authentic. According to Kenning, conscious investors need to take three steps:

1. Screen businesses for best practices and ESG criteria to understand what is beneath that as well
2. Engage with the investments that we are already making, including voting proxies
3. Invest in private markets so that those solutions can become more available on public markets later on

In the meantime, her advice is simple: know what you own, and think about where your cash is held.[107] Become conscious of your investments. There are countless examples of companies creating products that are used every day, such as Facebook, that may not operate from a reliable moral compass. Know where your money is sleeping at night and take steps to bring it into alignment with your values. If you already consider yourself a conscious investor, be flexible. Know when to adapt. Be mindful of how much you can take on. This is a *global* movement, separate from philanthropy and not at all restricted to the wealthiest members of society.

As you begin sorting through what you own, consider using all the resources listed in this book to make proactive choices to invest in companies that are *active* about their impact. We should be able to identify our values and find others who are working on and investing in those same issues. This is not about giving the most but about aligning the most with who we are and what we care about.

One year, Kenning took some of her clients to Africa to visit twelve different social enterprises. On that trip, she realized that her clients *wanted* to invest in those kinds of enterprises, but they felt trapped by the existing structure of investment. Meeting the women who have benefitted from her clients' investments and seeing the impact in action changed their perspective as a group. Her clients were more apt to get involved in social enterprises directly, and Kenning still looks back on that experience as a reason for why she does the work that she does.

From my own hands-on experience with Beyond Capital, those meetings are humanizing. They remind us why the intentionality behind our money is important. They remind us that great impact is just an investment away. And that we are, truly, all connected.

CHAPTER 9

be a discerning consumer and active citizen

n the introduction to this book, I described an event in Brussels
I attended in October 2016. At this event, I met a stylish couple
who had run some businesses for Louis Vuitton Moet Hennessy
(LVMH). They were French and had moved to Brussels for the tax
break the country offered to French expats. As we talked over incredible canapes, they shared a perspective that I will never forget.

"Philanthropy is the new luxury good."

I should not have been as surprised to hear that as I was. In reality,
they were merely summing up how so many people with privilege

have looked at social change—as a luxury reserved for the exceptionally rich, as a status symbol, something nice to have, but also easily done without. They were summing up the zeitgeist of the moment amid a bull market run of almost ten years.

As I write this four years later, I see some positive signs that society is starting to consider capital as a force for good. In fact, this aspiration has given rise to a new type of leader, the conscious leader, who actively practices servant leadership, considers all stakeholders, and promotes a philosophy of moral and ethical capitalism. Conscious leaders like Paul Polman, formerly of Unilever, and Russell Diez-Canseco, President and CEO of Vital Farms, are making conscious leadership even more popular and sought after—and in so doing, offering proof that conscious investing goes beyond the idea of philanthropy as a luxury good by putting primacy on the power of everyday actions instead. Investing becomes a holistic tool, a practical means of accomplishing goals, something we can (and should) talk about at the dinner table with our families. We have the opportunity to become discerning consumers and active citizens in every aspect of our lives but especially with our money.

According to Sean Hinton, who runs the Soros Economic Development Fund, we must manifest our values and beliefs in a full range of economic transactions. We should move away from the idea of a transactional world driven by only money to one that also integrates purpose. Hinton believes our responsibility is wider than ourselves, and we should take care not only in our investments but also our purchases and even our taxes.[108]

This raises some important questions: How can we use every part of our lives to support the kinds of change we want to see? How can we integrate our hearts and our heads to find meaning and purpose? Being a discerning consumer and active citizen means fully walking the talk.

Throughout this book, I have focused on the importance of the integration of the heart and head in every decision we make. While impact investing offers a clear path toward making this goal a reality, there are still opportunities to take this effort further. In this final chapter, we will examine the importance of becoming a discerning consumer and active citizen—and the many ways you can make your voice heard.

conscious consumerism

The operative word in impact investing—the *impact*—can happen in ways that are not characterized as traditional investing. You can make an impact by considering your power in what you choose or choose not to purchase. You can be more discerning about what you purchase and the companies you support. You can take a moment to research all your options, whether it is for a bottle of detergent or a new desk chair.

These are the concepts at the heart of conscious consumerism. One of the most important actions you can take to effect social change is to choose where you spend your money with care. With the unparalleled privilege of choice in what you buy and invest in comes a responsibility to consider the narratives. In service of that goal, asking questions always helps:

- Of the many options available, which companies are putting people, environment, and ethics first?
- Which options are B Corporations (which presupposes that the company balances purpose and profit)?
- Who are the leaders running the company, and what stands behind their social or environmental goals?

While many businesses make it easy to practice conscious consumerism, many other companies fall somewhere in the middle. Nike, for instance, does excellent work in some areas but leaves something to be desired in others. Specifically, while the company has changed its labor practices and was one of the first companies to align with Colin Kaepernick and the Black Lives Matter movement, they also do not use sustainable materials to produce their shoes.

To support a company like Nike, then, is to face the same dilemma that my husband and I have faced with our investment management firm. Is it more important to be fully aligned as a conscious consumer, or is it okay to support a company that is doing some good today and has potential to do better in the future?

The choice is yours. To guide that decision, ask: What is most important to you as a consumer? In terms of Nike, do you value sustainable environmental practices more or ethical labor practices and social justice?

Take the time to think about your specific values and what is important to you. Then, project those values onto the companies you are thinking of purchasing from. See if the company's values match yours and how you feel about supporting their behavior, good or bad, with your money. You have the ability to impact the world one small decision at a time. When you take the time to see your choices' impact beyond just the material good or service, it is like building a muscle. You will begin to see consumer choices in terms of what is most important for you to support and what is not resonant.

HOW MUCH IS ENOUGH?

In the area of conscious consumerism, my friend and colleague, Brent Kessel of Abacus Wealth, encourages his clients to think not only of what is right but where they can have the most impact in all areas. He asks: How much is enough? Where can you most easily make a difference? He personally uses these questions as a filter for decision-making throughout his life.[109] Switching to cloth napkins and water filters over bottled water does not require huge sacrifices but can create a meaningful impact over the long term. Similarly, if you only have so much time to research your consumer choices, spend that time on making ethical choices in the largest purchases first, like real estate. A new house powered entirely by solar energy could have a much larger impact than a pair of sustainable shoes will.[110] Asking the fundamental question of how much is enough also gives the opportunity to think differently about what we own and what we may not actually need to live happily and with meaning and purpose.

EVALUATING ALL STAKEHOLDERS

Do you know who all the stakeholders of your purchases are? Who and what are directly or indirectly impacted by a recent purchase?

Going back to the example of a company like Nike, the company has a significant environmental impact because it sells at scale, and its shoes get recycled only so many times before ending up in landfills. Nike's employees, both in manufacturing and office jobs, are all affected by company policies, including employee benefits and diversity policies.

Investors and suppliers also see tremendous impact from Nike, as do the communities in which they run their operations. The consumers and the values of consumers are also impacted by the products themselves and the advertising around those products. Nike makes many admirable choices, but the company's environmental impact is not perfect, and its products would not align well with a consumer primarily focused on climate action and environmental conservation.

It is important, however, not to let perfect be the enemy of good. Companies that listen are good potential allies, and you can continue to influence them as a consumer to act responsibly across the board. Do not dismiss companies that make imperfect efforts; keep pushing them to do more.

Your highest-priority value should drive your decisions in the companies you purchase from and choose to support. You will feel good about the values you are integrating into your purchasing habits, and the feeling and impact will add up.

For instance, if the environment is a core area of focus as a conscious consumer, then you may want to choose a brand like Patagonia, Allbirds, or United by Blue instead of Nike. United by Blue is an outdoor brand with a fully sustainable supply chain. The "Blue" in the company's name refers to the ocean, and their campaign around the ocean and conservation sits at the core of their business. United by Blue has pledged that for each product purchased, they will pay to have one pound of ocean trash removed.

United by Blue has also developed its own fabrics, many of which are made out of durable hemp. This focus on sustainable materials has also led them to expand their product offerings in recent years as well. The company is a great example of what I like to call "walking the talk" rather than being an ally solely for optics and marketing. Choosing a company like United by Blue not only supports the business and marine conservation, but it also puts pressure on less purpose-driven companies like Nike (with your wallet) to compete at a similar level. Conscious consumerism is just activism by another name.[111]

VOTING WITH YOUR SHARES

When I was a child, friends and family gave paper bonds to children for birthdays, communions, bat mitzvahs, graduations, and other life milestones. I would receive a bond in a company, and even at a young age, I would feel a tangible feeling of ownership. Now, the bonds and stocks in our portfolios are stored electronically and traded on electronic exchanges. Investing, to a large degree, has forgotten the idea and feeling that owning a share entitles you to a voice.

And yet, as activist hedge fund managers and activist shareholders have taught me in my careers, we absolutely *do* have a voice. When I was working in the hedge fund industry, I had the opportunity to invest in and engage with many activist hedge fund managers. These are managers who buy a stake in a company and then use that stake to push for change. Often in the financial industry, the change they want relates solely to the financial bottom line, though in recent years investors have been asking for more as well.

Over a decade ago, seeing the activist hedge fund managers in action got me thinking about how to influence companies as a conscious investor. One way is through owning stock in a company. Shareholders have a vote in the affairs of the companies they own. Proxy voting, where you or your broker will vote your voting shares on specific issues, is critically important. (The vote is referred to as a proxy vote because shareholders do not typically attend in-person shareholder meetings.) Common questions that come to a vote are share ownership, the structure of the board of directors, executive salary, and many ESG issues, such as lobbying disclosure, climate change, and data privacy. Even with a limited range of topics, proxy voting can still become a form of impact activism. If you know there are not enough women or people of color on the board of directors or the executive is paying himself millions and treating employees unfairly, your vote can have a considerable impact. For instance, you could vote on a binding resolution that could influence the company's direction. However, you have to actively express that vote, which is often like the tick of a box or an indication to your financial advisor that you want to vote your proxy. Simply put, not voting is having ownership in a business without paying attention to how it is being run and who is running it.

We have moved so far away from the idea of real company ownership that it is easy to think shareholders do not have a voice. But we do. When we own part of a company, we also have the right to engage with that company and make it better for the future. You can also track how the funds in your portfolio vote across different ESG issues.

Many find it acceptable to work within the system, pushing for change in their ways. You have the freedom to develop your own strategy. For instance, you could choose to support B Corporations and companies that already do good in a holistic way, which forces the financial system to place a higher value on all stakeholders and ESG.

taxation as a way to contribute beyond yourself

I am sure that some reading this book dislike paying their taxes. While I have given thought to the idea of tax optimization in the past, in the same way I think about where my money sleeps at night, I also approach my taxes as a social responsibility that I am proud of. Taxes buy security and peace of mind. It is a privilege to be able to contribute to something bigger than myself, and I do not believe that government inefficiency is a reason to decide not to pay for public goods.

Whether we acknowledge it, we are all part of—and benefit from—a larger society. I live in a country that has functioning roads, laws, and far more public resources than many of the countries in which I invest through Beyond Capital. My taxes contributed, for example, to the extra $600 a week in unemployment benefits that Americans received during the COVID-19 pandemic, money that for some was the difference between being food secure or going hungry. Do not lose sight of how lucky we are to have the opportunity to contribute *to* our society.

the power of the consumer

In the book *Inconspicuous Consumption: The Environmental Impact You Don't Know You Have,* author Tatiana Schlossberg describes her surprise at learning the environmental impact of denim. As Schlossberg learned, denim manufacturing is an extremely water-intensive process. It takes a full two thousand gallons of water to grow just two pounds of cotton, and turning cotton into a pair of jeans can use up to 2,900 more gallons of water in addition to that. For perspective, these numbers represent 3 percent of all agricultural freshwater usage globally.[112]

This is not to say that it was her fault that she did not know the impact of denim production. Schlossberg flatly rejects that idea. As she argues, consumers are often shamed for making choices that go against our values. "It is really hard for the average consumer to know that," Schlossberg says, "and I don't think that it should be on each one of us to figure out which pair of jeans was produced with the least water. It is the responsibility of the companies to take more responsibility for the supply chain and adopt practices to dramatically reduce the amount of water they use."[113] While, in 2020, I myself decided to stop my personal consumption of denim, there is choice in where and how to source materials to produce denim more responsibly.

However, an essential mindset of wealth consciousness is taking stock of what you currently own. And once you do know what you own and what you are supporting with your consumer dollars, you cannot unknow it. You become responsible for that choice, aware of what you want to consume, and aware of the differences between choices in everyday purchases and large-scale financial decisions.

Global supply chain integration—the way that large companies operate with a number of suppliers, in multiple countries, with various sourcing, purchasing, and labor tactics—has blurred the lines of accountability. Hans Stegeman, Head of Investment Strategy and Research for Triodos Investment, explained that:

> For almost all technological equipment such as smartphones, cars, laptops, and TVs, it has become virtually impossible for the average consumer or investor to determine where and under what circumstances parts are produced and where the raw materials are sourced; therefore, the clear link with the real economy has become much more obscure due to the development of global value chains.[114]

You cannot be expected to know how every company produces every product you buy, but you can work to make better decisions with the information that is available to you.

Schlossberg looked further into a sneaker company called Allbirds, which produces all of their fabrics in a more sustainable way. They have even made the fabric blend open source for other companies to use as well, thereby helping to develop a larger market of sustainable brands. Of course, Allbirds has a strategic business reason for making their fabric open source. The more demand there is for sustainably produced fabrics, the lower their production costs become. Regardless, they found a way to create something good and leapt at the opportunity. Our decisions to support or not support companies like Allbirds is important—not just for them but for the way other companies behave as well.

Anecdotally, this resonates with my own decisions as a consumer. When I chose to use Lyft over Uber whenever possible, I did so for two reasons: First was the fact that I have had numerous bad experiences with Uber drivers. Second was the growing body of reports describing a company that did not treat its drivers well and ignored claims of abuse among riders. No wonder I had so many bad experiences! With this knowledge, I could not, in good conscience, support that company. Since then, my experience with Lyft has been exemplary, reflecting a company whose stated values are more aligned with my own.[115]

When enough people take a stand for their convictions, it has a ripple effect that reaches the highest levels of business. Take, for example, the 2019 Business Roundtable announcement stating that corporations have responsibilities beyond their shareholders and to society at large.[116] That is a seismic shift if you consider the immense role companies play in society, and it shows the power you have as an individual in holding them accountable. Consider, then, just how much power you hold as a conscious investor determined to bring businesses into accountability across all areas.

Your dollars matter. The money you spend as a consumer influences companies. You should not only expect more from your money, but you should also ask more from the companies you are buying from. I personally have a list of companies I will not ever buy from, whose policies I will not support. I am sure that you may have a mental list as well. Using your voice and your money more consciously will aid in exceeding what your portfolio can do.

I am sure you have come across the idea of voting with your money before. As Schlossberg says, we as consumers are not causing the damage ourselves, and we should not necessarily blame ourselves. You can certainly change your habits. But more importantly, the companies you buy from should take more responsibility. Knowing your power in asking more as a consumer can help spur those companies to take action.

active involvement

In 1999, I was growing up in New York City when a Black man named Amadou Diallo was killed. I was still a child, so when I heard the story on the news, I asked my parents about it. I was so disturbed by what they told me that my mother encouraged me to write a letter to *The New York Times* editorial board, which for me was a local newspaper. The letter was never published, but I learned that day the importance of using my voice.

Up to this point, I have talked mainly about the power you have in the choices you make with your money. However, you also have time, skills, education, and even the way we frame arguments to shape change. As Lisa Kleissner says about the financial industry, we need to collectively ask for more. I will continue to find ways to work toward gender and racial equality, better solutions for the environment, ubiquity of education, and poverty alleviation both in my professional and personal lives.

It is all too common to let life get busy. Then, you wake up one day and realize that your money sleeps in a bank that is a major financier of coal production, a practice that directly contradicts your values related to global climate change!

It is imperative to think about the system in which we operate. Further, we need to think about what we actually stand for, reclaim our power, and reshape conversations about the environment we want to live in. For instance, have you ever realized how strange it is that someone who espouses racial equality, environmental steward-ship, or women's rights is considered an *activist*? Not only are these commonly held values, but they are far from radial concepts in the twenty-first century.

Sustainable business is not just an expression of values; as you now know, it is also a viable investment strategy. As Jon Hale notes in an analysis of ESG data, sustainable investing delivers competitive performance on an ongoing basis in both up and down markets. However, Hale stresses that the greater purpose of sustainable investing is to incentivize companies to adopt a long-term, stakeholder-centric model that benefits both people and the planet.[117]

Investors who care about change often think that by investing money, they are supporting the system that created the problems they are solving for. However, if I become an activist with my money, if I work to collectively out the system for its existing impact, and if I push to integrate social and environmental values into invest-ing, then I might actually have a chance at changing systems for the benefit of everyone. Moreover, I will likely produce financial return along the way and be able to reuse the capital, which should make the impact longer-lasting than one-time philanthropy with the same money.

CIVIC ENGAGEMENT

Old-school environmentalism was mainly about planting trees, saving the polar bears, and picking up trash. As I shared earlier, my family has a history in politics. My uncle, David Bonior, made it a point of his campaign to send tree saplings to voters. He would then host tree planting days to symbolize his devotion to the environment and how he would vote in Congress. These events became not just about galvanizing support but also about engaging with and inspiring the community.

My uncle's campaign inspired me to think differently. Where I put my money is such a private and quiet decision; nobody sees my investment portfolio but me. Wearing my values on my sleeve, however, whether it is writing to *The New York Times* editorial board or reducing my consumption, can inspire others and further my goals in ways that quiet decisions do not.

It is for these reasons that I admire fashion entrepreneur Suzanne Lerner so much. Lerner exemplifies the notion of acting in accordance with one's values. When Lerner founded her company, Michael Stars, which became a well-known brand in the eighties, she did so with the value of women's equality foremost in her mind. Aside from using her status as CEO to amplify her voice, Lerner also reflects her values in other ways. Her company, Michael Stars, for instance, produces T-shirts with the statement "Feminism Is for Everybody." Further, her investment portfolio is 100 percent aligned with her values.

Suzanne does not stop there, however. She is politically active as well. She wants to help change policy, to make a difference for diversity in corporations and gender rights across the board. With her political activism, she supports LGBTQ+ rights and racial equality as well. Her active citizenry work has become a natural extension of her values in the same way her business and portfolio are. Now, you can benefit from her example by applying her approach to multiple areas of your life.[118]

EMPLOYEES HAVE INFLUENCE TOO

I remember seeing an advertisement in a business magazine for a company that helped businesses appeal to millennial employees. The advertisement reminded me that employees have more influence than they often think. Business can often be driven by the status quo.

If you work for a company, you can have a tremendous impact by advocating for business practices that promote environmental sustainability or social consciousness, for example. Advocating for change from within can be an incredible way to further your social goals and even further the mission of the company. Employees raising their hands was how the investment firm BlackRock became the Wall Street industry leader in sustainable investing. If there is something you are passionate about that you think could also be a business strategy at the company you are working at, be willing to volunteer to lead the charge.

CREATIVE TOOLS

One of my favorite artists is Ai Wei Wei, a Chinese activist whose work is extraordinarily beautiful. He makes activism part of his work, integrating history and injustices as subject matter, and has worked with artists across the globe to create documentaries on human rights abuses. Most of his work has a strong political theme, and that theme is expressed through a combination of explaining history and current events using historical objects and iconography. Ai Wei Wei underlines human rights violations as a way to push boundaries and has been jailed several times. In fact, so powerful was his work and so consistent was his commitment that at one point he could no longer live in China.

Activism does not always have to be writing a letter, making an argument, or attending a protest. Protesting, demonstrating, and signing petitions are incredible ways to make change. However, they are not the only options. There are many ways to be an activist.

As a photographer, Jaime Miller is focused on making people feel seen and empowered. This emphasis gave rise to what Miller calls "The Gifted Project," a movement that celebrates and honors Black men by showing them in a more positive light through portraiture. What I love about her activism through her artwork is that she is using art as a medium to try and change the worldview of a particular type of person in the United States, who is heavily stereotyped and is the recipient of significant bias. Many other artists in the United States have also raised awareness about critical social issues with their work, including Nick Cave, Nneka Jones, and Calida Garcia-Rawles.[119]

your voice counts

It took me a while to move away from the ivory tower and to shake off the hierarchical thinking I learned in finance. Everyone has a voice, and that voice is about more than just the money you have. Using that voice in more than one area of your life is how you will yield the biggest results toward your goals.

I realized that the social and environmental outcomes I wanted to see were not, in fact, fringe. They are normal asks of society. In realizing this, I had more freedom. I could see that the change I want is not a radical shift from the status quo. And being an activist—caring about social and environmental impact—is not new. It should be seen as a normal, everyday behavior, not a radical thing to do. It is actually normal, a natural outgrowth of expressing our values authentically.

If you are a leader, one of the most powerful ways you can affect change is through conscious leadership. Be thoughtful about the holistic results of every decision that you make. Balance practical and purpose. Offer support and listen. Lead by example, regardless of how big or how small your platform might be.

We live at a time with abundant opportunities to do good. I am excited and inspired by the next generation and those who have come before us. The chance to affect change is open to all of us. Becoming a conscious investor is available to everyone.

NOW, LET YOUR MONEY DO GOOD

We are all looking for meaning and joy in our lives. What I have learned over the years is that consciousness empowers both the investor and the ultimate beneficiary. When Beyond Capital invested in ERC Eyecare, the portfolio earned an impressive return and set the company on course to serve over three hundred thousand customers a year. More importantly, Guna does not have to worry about his family or his business—he can access the eye care he needs and carry on with his daily life.

Because of Numida, Shafique does not have to choose between his daughter's education and growing the business that will pay for it in the future.

Because of Frontier Markets, Hina can walk through her village with her head held high, and the last-mile recipients of the products she sells can access the basic supplies they need for everyday life, even in rural areas.

Because of impact investing, there are millions of stories just like these. Some of them will motivate more investments that will serve more individuals and the environment. Some of them will never be told. They will simply find *saral jeevan*—an easy life—and carry on loving their families and caring for their neighbors. As their livelihoods improve and they begin to affect others, a wave of impact will swell that can never be measured or stopped.

hope is intentional

Money is not our only source of wealth. We can become wealthy relationally, spiritually, environmentally, and emotionally. And just as easily, we can become destitute. The difference is in how we invest in each of those areas.

Natasha Mueller, as a younger investor, is part of the generation who will continue to live with the side effects of climate change, like me and my children. In the face of this despair, hope has been her activator. It is not an intangible force but an intentional action. A choice to face what brings us despair and respond with whatever tools we have in our grasp.

Ian Walker of Left Coast Naturals has lived out his purpose through every level of business growth for nearly twenty-five years.

Shah stretched her passion for empowering rural women beyond surface levels and has been able to employ thousands of females while still moving the needle on last-mile distribution.

Jeffrey Brown is employing the unemployable, Rosalie is delivering women their essential needs that had been inaccessible—and individuals like Mathilde, Brian, and the Beyond Capital team are finding joy in supporting them all.

It has been incredible to watch communities come together, offering up energy, money, and time as a force for good. This approach to investing has given me lifelong friends, personal growth, and a strong network. It has made me a more authentic person. Even my college friends and former Wall Street colleagues have reconnected with me through this work—one has volunteered twenty hours of his time a month to help with evaluating portfolio companies for Beyond Capital.

In writing this book, I have realized the immense power of asking questions across all the decisions we make and how much that can influence us toward being more conscious. In asking these questions, it is important for us to not be judgmental or dogmatic but to be generous with ourselves in listening to what the answers are and learning from them.

Finally, I cannot quantify what impact investing has brought me, my family, and my husband. It will not fit on a spreadsheet. I am happier, mentally and physically healthier, and more fulfilled. I do not feel hopeless or powerless in the face of great social problems or restrictive traditional finance rules.

By empowering others, I have personally become empowered. Now, it is your turn.

SDGs

Mentions	Chapter/Section	SDGs Mentioned
Natasha Mueller	1/Natasha's Story	Goals 7, 13
Keren Eldad	1/Beyond Capital—Bold Financial Investments	Goal 3
Ian Walker	2/Introduction	Goals 3, 11, 12, 13, 15
Frontier Markets	2/Looking for Saral Jeevan	Goals 1, 5, 7, 8, 10
Ajaita Shah	2/Ajaita's Story	Goals 1, 5, 7, 10
Dan Price	2/Enlightened Self-Interest	Goal 8
ERC Eye Care	2/The Power of Experience	Goal 3
Jeffrey Brown	3/Jeffrey's Story	Goals 2, 3, 10, 11
Revolution Foods	3/Find Your Cause	Goals 2, 3, 4, 12
East Africa Fruit Farms	3/Is Doing Good Good Enough?	Goal 1, 15
Kasha	4/Rosalie's Impact	Goals 1, 3, 5, 8
Karma Healthcare	4/Impact in Action	Goal 3
Second Muse	5/Taking Action	Goals 10, 12
Greenworks Lending	5/Taking Action	Goals 9, 11, 13
Avangard Innovative	5/Taking Action	Goal 12
Arlan Hamilton	5/Examine Your Implicit Bias	Goals 5, 8, 10
Lisa Kleissner	6/Introduction	Goals 14, 17

acknowledgments

After over a decade as an impact investor, I have observed that when it comes to purpose, people are everything in bringing meaning to life.

Writing a book has been the perfect opportunity to share the depth of experience I have been privileged to acquire as an investor with a lens toward social and environmental returns.

I am most grateful to my husband and Beyond Capital cofounder, Hooman Yazhari, who has supported me in every area of my life since the day we met in 2008. Equality has been at the core of our relationship since the start. It represents our values as a couple and family, providing the foundation on which we view our impact.

To Alessandro and Aurelia, through your lives, I get to see how lucky I truly am to exist.

I am also grateful to my parents and my family, who taught me that I have the duty to emphasize social justice over the pure pursuit of money and to always better the system in which I operate.

To the Beyond Capital Team, who has diligently supported and nurtured our portfolio companies and mission of improving the livelihoods of millions of individuals.

To Mathilde—I am hopeful that the deep caring your generation embraces will change the world.

To Coach Keren Eldad and my personal high-vibe tribe, who have encouraged me to think beyond the lenses of impact investing and venture capital and have inspired joyful creativity in my life.

To Ed Stevens—working on *The Beyond Capital Podcast* is informative, inspiring, and fun. Without our podcast interviews with purpose-driven entrepreneurs, many of the anecdotes of conscious leaders in this book would not be possible.

My dream of inspiring a wider audience to become conscious investors came true when I launched *The Conscious Investor* with Stacey Lindsay. Stacey's journalism talent has incited an approachable yet informative tone in our magazine, which further motivated me to share how anyone can become a conscious investor.

There are thousands of impact investors who have stood up to say that financial return was not enough for their portfolios; in doing so, they created a new way for us all to invest. I have deep gratitude for the pioneers who blazed the trail to have this important conversation and the new wave of conscious investors who will continue to demand more from their money.

Lastly, turning an idea into a book has been both internally challenging and rewarding, and it has taken time and resources. I especially want to thank Chas Hoppe—we could not have been better aligned as partners on this project.

about the author

Eva Yazhari is a seasoned investor, entrepreneur, and CEO with sixteen years of experience working in the venture capital and asset management industries. She is the cofounder and CEO of Beyond Capital, a pioneering impact investing fund dedicated to the belief that investing can inspire good and sustainably improve access to basic goods and services. She also cohosts the podcast *The Beyond Capital Podcast*.

Eva launched a weekly magazine, *The Conscious Investor*, in 2019. She has appeared in interviews with the lifestyle brands Goop and Thrive Global and in Authority Magazine and Cheddar. She also has been a guest on numerous podcasts and a speaker at office, family, and impact investing conferences.

Eva lives in Dallas, Texas, with her family.

notes

1   Jen Sincero, *You Are a Badass: How to Stop Doubting Your Greatness and Start Living an Awesome Life* (Philadelphia: Running Press, 2013).

2   Yuval Noah Harari, *Sapiens: A Brief History of Humankind* (New York: Harper, 2015).

3   Martin Seligman, *Authentic Happiness: Using the New Positive Psychology to Realize Your Potential for Lasting Fulfillment* (New York: Atria, 2004).

4   For further reading, see my Q&A in Goop: "Conscious Money: The Double Returns of Impact Investing," 2019, https://goop.com/work/civics/conscious-money-the-double-returns-of-impact-investing/.

5   Neil Irwin, "Growth Has Been Good for Decades. So Why Hasn't Poverty Declined?" *The New York Times*, June 4, 2014, https://www.nytimes.com/2014/06/05/upshot/growth-has-been-good-for-decades-so-why-hasnt-poverty-declined.html.

6   William F. Meehan III, "Philanthropy: Not the Problem, Not the Solution," *Forbes*, October 25, 2019, https://www.forbes.com/sites/williammeehan/2019/10/25/philanthropy-not-the-problem-not-the-solution/?sh=5bdd781725d7.

7   David Callahan, "'Impossible to Justify.' A Political Scientist Takes on American Philanthropy," *Inside Philanthropy*, January 7, 2019, https://www.insidephilanthropy.com/home/2019/1/7/impossible-to-justify-a-political-scientist-takes-on-american-philanthropy.

8   The United Nations, "About the Sustainable Development Goals," Sustainable Development Goals, https://www.un.org/sustainabledevelopment/sustainable-development-goals/.

9   "Impactful Investing: Jessica Droste Yagan of Impact Engine," *The Beyond Capital Podcast*, January 21, 2020, https://www.beyondcapitalpodcast.com/blog/impact-engine.

10 "Impactful Investing: Jessica Droste Yagan of Impact Engine," *The Beyond Capital Podcast*, January 21, 2020, https://www.beyondcapitalpodcast.com/blog/impact-engine.

11 Alan Schwartz and Reuben Finighan, "Impact Investing Won't Save Capitalism," *Harvard Business Review*, July 17, 2020, https://hbr.org/2020/07/impact-investing-wont-save-capitalism.

12 "2020 Report on US Sustainable, Responsible, and Impact Investing Trends," US SIF Foundation, https://www.ussif.org/store_product.asp?prodid=42.

13 Abby Schultz, "Impact Investments Rise Amid COVID-19 Pandemic," *Barron's*, April 5, 2020, https://www.barrons.com/articles/impact-investments-rise-amid-covid-19-pandemic-01586086243.

14 "Sustainability: The Future of Investing," BlackRock Investment Institute, February 1, 2019, https://www.blackrock.com/us/individual/insights/blackrock-investment-institute/sustainability-the-future-of-investing.

15 Ron O'Hanley, "Investor Focus on Sustainability Is about Managing Risk," State Street, February 2020, https://www.statestreet.com/ideas/articles/investor-focus-on-sustainability-is-about-managing-risk.html.

16 Abhilash Mudaliar, Rachel Bass, Hannah Dithrich, and Noshin Nova, "2019 Annual Impact Investor Survey," Global Impact Investing Network, June 19, 2019, https://thegiin.org/research/publication/impinv-survey-2019.

17 Ibid.

18 Robert G. Eccles, Ioannis Ioannou, and George Serafeim, "The Impact of Corporate Sustainability on Organizational Processes and Performance," Harvard Business School, 2014, https://www.hbs.edu/faculty/Publication%20Files/SSRN-id1964011_6791edac-7daa-4603-a220-4a0c6c7a3f7a.pdf.

19 Seventh Generation, "We're a Company on a Mission," 2020, https://www.seventhgeneration.com/insideSVG/mission.

20 Conscious Capitalism, 2020, https://www.consciouscapitalism.org/.

21 Gustavo Razzetti, "Your Success Depends on the Emotional Culture," *Psychology Today*, April 12, 2019, https://www.psychologytoday.com/us/blog/the-adaptive-mind/201904/your-success-depends-the-emotional-culture.

22 Kristin Broughton and Maitane Sardon, "Coronavirus Pandemic Could Elevate ESG Factors," *The Wall Street Journal*, March 25, 2020, https://www.wsj.com/articles/coronavirus-pandemic-could-elevate-esg-factors-11585167518.

23 Thomas H. Stoner Jr. and David Schimel, "Opinion: Coronavirus Will Realign Investors' Priorities Toward a New Normal of Sustainability," *MarketWatch*, March 20, 2020, https://www.marketwatch.com/story/coronavirus-will-realign-investors-priorities-toward-a-new-normal-of-sustainability-2020-03-20.

24 Larissa Basso, "Why a 17% Emissions Drop Does Not Mean We Are Addressing Climate Change," *World Economic Forum*, May 27, 2020, https://

www.weforum.org/agenda/2020/05/why-a-17-emissions-drop-does-not-mean-we-are-addressing-climate-change/.

25   Rebecca Suhrawardi, "How Do Consumers Feel about Fashion During Coronavirus? Here's What AI Thinks," *Forbes*, April 10, 2020, https://www.forbes.com/sites/rebeccasuhrawardi/2020/04/10/how-do-consumers-feel-about-fashion-during-coronavirus-heres-what-ai-thinks/ - 3d0f860d419d.

26   Just Capital, "The COVID-19 Corporate Response Tracker: How America's Largest Employers Are Treating Stakeholders Amid the Coronavirus Crisis," 2020, https://justcapital.com/reports/the-covid-19-corporate-response-tracker-how-americas-largest-employers-are-treating-stakeholders-amid-the-coronavirus-crisis/.

27   Just Capital, "Here's How Companies Are Serving Their Stakeholders During the Coronavirus Crisis," March 24, 2020, https://justcapital.com/news/heres-how-companies-are-serving-their-stakeholders-during-the-coronavirus-crisis/.

28   Robert Livingston, "How to Promote Racial Equity in the Workplace," *Harvard Business Review*, September–October, 2020, https://hbr.org/2020/09/how-to-promote-racial-equity-in-the-workplace.

29   It is worth noting that these numbers were pre-COVID. Estimates after the pandemic may be dramatically different.

30   "Beneficial Snacks: Ian Walker of Left Coast Naturals," *The Beyond Capital Podcast*, November 12, 2019, https://www.beyondcapitalpodcast.com/blog/beneficial-snacks.

31   Fidelity, "Study: 77% of Millennials have Made an Impact Investment, but Only 53% of Advisors Understand the Concept Well," 2020, https://www.fidelitycharitable.org/about-us/news/77-percent-millennials-made-impact-investment-only-53-percent-advisors-say-they-understand-concept-well.html.

32   Deep Patel, "Eight Ways that Generation Z Will Differ from Millennials in the Workplace," *Forbes*, September 17, 2017, https://www.forbes.com/sites/deeppatel/2017/09/21/8-ways-generation-z-will-differ-from-millennials-in-the-workplace/ - 27d652b876e5.

33   Ann Gherini, "Gen-Z Is About to Outnumber Millennials. Here's How That Will Affect the Business World," *Inc.* August 22, 2018, https://www.inc.com/anne-gherini/gen-z-is-about-to-outnumber-millennials-heres-how-that-will-affect-business-world.html.

34   Shawn Achor, "Positive Intelligence," *Harvard Business Review*, 2012, https://hbr.org/2012/01/positive-intelligence.

35   David Steindl-Rast, "Want to Be Happy? Be Grateful," TEDGlobal, 2013, https://www.ted.com/talks/david_steindl_rast_want_to_be_happy_be_grateful/up-next?language=en.

36 Joshua Weisner, "5 Intrinsic Benefits of Helping Others," Goalcast, December 16, 2016, https://www.goalcast.com/2016/12/11/5-intrinsic-benefits-helping-others/.

37 Shannon Mehner, "Kindness Is Contagious, New Study Finds," Helix, April 21, 2010, https://helix.northwestern.edu/article/kindness-contagious-new-study-finds.

38 The World Bank, "Social Safety Net Programs Help Millions Escape Poverty, But Coverage Gaps Persist," April 4, 2018, https://www.worldbank.org/en/news/press-release/2018/04/04/social-safety-net-programs-help-millions-escape-poverty-but-coverage-gaps-persist.

39 "Supporting Small Business: Dan Price of Gravity Payments," May 12, 2020, *The Beyond Capital Podcast*, https://www.beyondcapitalpodcast.com/blog/supporting-small-business.

40 Brené Brown, *Dare to Lead: Brave Work. Tough Conversations. Whole Hearts.* (London: Vermilion, 2018).

41 Rebecca Henderson, "Does Capitalism Need to Be Reimagined?" *Harvard Magazine*, November 16, 2020, https://harvardmagazine.com/2020/rebecca-henderson.

42 Each of them gives anywhere between twenty-five to thirty hours a month, which equates to a total of $550,000 a year.

43 Andrew Steptoe and Daisy Fancourt, "Leading a Meaningful Life at Older Ages and Its Relationship with Social Engagement, Prosperity, Health, Biology, and Time Use," *Proceedings of the National Academy of Sciences of the United States of America*, January 7, 2019, https://doi.org/10.1073/pnas.1814723116.

44 "Why We Need Radical Cultural Solutions to Overcome the World's Most Pressing Challenges," The Conscious Investor, December 26, 2019, https://www.theconsciousinvestor.co/blog/michael-vlerick.

45 For more on Mr. Vlerick's perspective, see: https://www.theconsciousinvestor.co/blog/michael-vlerick.

46 Personal communication, April 16, 2020.

47 Impact Alpha, "Week of September 11th," *Impact Briefing*, September 11, 2020, https://podcasts.apple.com/us/podcast/impact-briefing/id1499524658?i=1000490898421.

48 For an overview of Ariely's findings, see Oliver Staley, "Four Ways to Motivate Employees, According to a Top Behavioral Economist," *Quartz at Work*, January 3, 2017, https://qz.com/work/875401/four-ways-to-better-motivate-your-employees-from-one-of-the-worlds-most-prominent-behavioral-economists/. For a more complete presentation of his findings, see Ariely's book, *Payoff: The Hidden Logic That Shapes Our Motivations*, http://danariely.com/books/payoff/.

49 Raj Raghunathan, "Why Rich People Aren't as Happy as They Could Be," *Harvard Business Review*, June 8, 2016, https://hbr.org/2016/06/why-rich-people-arent-as-happy-as-they-could-be.

50 The United Nations, "UN Secretary-General's Strategy for Financing the 2030 Agenda," Sustainable Development Goals, https://www.un.org/sustainabledevelopment/sg-finance-strategy/.

51 Dean Hand, et. al., "2020 Annual Impact Investor Survey," Global Impact Investing Network, June 11, 2020, https://thegiin.org/research/publication/impinv-survey-2020.

52 "The $26 Trillion Opportunity," World Resources Institute, https://www.wri.org/blog-series/the-26-trillion-opportunity.

53 A. Hammond, et. al., *The Next 4 Billion*, World Resources Institute, 2007, https://www.wri.org/publication/next-4-billion.

54 To learn more about Jeffrey's work, see: "Good Food: Jeffrey Brown of Brown's Super Stores," *The Beyond Capital Podcast*, October 22, 2019, https://www.beyondcapitalpodcast.com/blog/good-food-jeffrey-brown-of-browns-super-stores.

55 T.H. Chan School of Public Health, "Child Obesity," Harvard University, 2020, https://www.hsph.harvard.edu/obesity-prevention-source/obesity-trends/global-obesity-trends-in-children/.

56 Lauren Bauer, "About 14 Million Children in the US Are Not Getting Enough to Eat," Brookings, July 9, 2020, https://www.brookings.edu/blog/up-front/2020/07/09/about-14-million-children-in-the-us-are-not-getting-enough-to-eat/.

57 Michael L. Anderson, Justin Gallagher, and Elizabeth Ramirez Ritchie, "School Meal Quality and Academic Performance," University of California, Berkeley, CA, October 23, 2018, https://are.berkeley.edu/~mlanderson/pdf/school_lunch.pdf.

58 The United Nations, "'We Face a Global Emergency' Over Oceans: UN Chief Sounds the Alarm at G7 Summit Event," June 9, 2018, https://news.un.org/en/story/2018/06/1011811.

59 Carmen Reinicke, "Bank of America: These Are the Top 10 Reasons Investors and Companies Should Care about ESG Investing," *Business Insider*, September 26, 2019, https://markets.businessinsider.com/news/stocks/10-reasons-to-care-about-esg-investing-bank-of-america-2019-9-1028557439#.

60 Ryan Gorman, "Women Now Control More Than Half of US Personal Wealth, Which 'Will Only Increase in Years to Come,'" *Business Insider*, April 7, 2015, https://www.businessinsider.com/women-now-control-more-than-half-of-us-personal-wealth-2015-4.

61 Jenny Gross, "Wealthy Millennial Women Tend to Defer to Husbands on Investing," *The New York Times*, October 24, 2020, https://www.nytimes.com/2020/10/24/business/millennial-personal-finance.html.

62 Joshua Brockman, "Women Are 'Claiming Their Power' in Investment Clubs of Their Own," *The New York Times*, April 24, 2020, https://www.nytimes.com/2020/04/24/business/women-investing-clubs-retirement.html.

63 For more on the efforts of Sallie Krawcheck and Ellevest, see Joshua Brockman, "Women Are 'Claiming Their Power' in Investment Clubs of Their Own," *The New York Times*, April 24, 2020, https://www.nytimes.com/2020/04/24/business/women-investing-clubs-retirement.html; Lindsey Taylor Wood, "Sallie Krawcheck of Ellevest: Her Fight to Close the Gender Investing Gap," The Helm, January 19, 2018, https://www.thehelm.co/sallie-krawcheck-gender-investing-gap/; and Ellevest, https://www.ellevest.com/.

64 Jason Hartman, "Meet the Female Leaders of Finance," *Authority Magazine*, November 21, 2019, https://medium.com/authority-magazine/meet-the-female-leaders-of-finance-we-need-to-reframe-the-conversation-about-money-to-be-more-ff718df04495.

65 Trish Costello, "Women Are Hacking Venture Capital, and People Don't See It Coming," Mattermark, February 26, 2016, https://mattermark.com/women-are-hacking-venture-capital-and-the-guys-dont-see-it-coming/.

66 Isabel Wilkerson, "Caste: The Origins of Our Discontents," Audible Live, August 4, 2020, https://www.audible.com/ep/audible-live-featuring-isabel-wilkerson.

67 Andrew Steptoe and Daisy Fancourt, "Leading a Meaningful Life at Older Ages and Its Relationship with Social Engagement, Prosperity, Health, Biology, and Time Use," *Proceedings of the National Academy of Sciences of the United States of America*, January 7, 2019, https://doi.org/10.1073/pnas.1814723116.

68 Hooman Yazhari, "The CEO Mindset: The Secret to Being a Successful and Empowering Leader," The Conscious Investor, February 26, 2020, https://www.theconsciousinvestor.co/blog/ceo-mindset-hooman-yazhari.

69 Stacey Lindsay, "My Moral Compass: Venture Capitalist Arlan Hamilton Is Amplifying the Talent and Power of 'Underestimated' Founders," The Conscious Investor, September 24, 2020, https://www.theconsciousinvestor.co/blog/arlan-hamilton-founder-backstage-capital.

70 Cliff Worley, "The Venture Capital World Has a Problem with Women of Color," Kapor Capital, April 12, 2019, https://www.kaporcapital.com/the-venture-capital-world-has-a-problem-with-women-of-color/.

71 For the full conversation, see: "Organizing for Good: Carrie Freeman of Second Muse," *The Beyond Capital Podcast*, November 19, 2019, https://www.beyondcapitalpodcast.com/blog/organizing-for-good.

72 For the full conversation, see: "Smart Money: Jessica Bailey of Greenworks Lending," *The Beyond Capital Podcast*, December 2, 2019, https://www.beyondcapitalpodcast.com/blog/greenworks.

73 For the full conversation, see: "The Circular Economy: Recycling Visionary Rick Perez," *The Beyond Capital Podcast*, October 24, 2019, https://www.beyondcapitalpodcast.com/blog/episode-2-the-circular-economy-recycling-visionary-rick-perez.

74 Jasmine Rashid, "The Financial Activist Playbook Supporting Black Lives," *Medium*, June 3, 2020, https://medium.com/candide-group/the-financial-activist-playbook-for-supporting-black-lives-fb9616470c4.

75 The Business Roundtable, https://www.businessroundtable.org/.

76 Lauren Smart, "ESG Meets Behavioral Finance: Part 1," Trucost, March 8, 2018, https://www.trucost.com/trucost-blog/esg-meets-behavioral-finance-part-1/.

77 Paul McCaffrey, "Meir Statman on Coronavirus, Behavioral Finance: The Second Generation, and More," Enterprising Investor, April 8, 2020, https://blogs.cfainstitute.org/investor/2020/04/08/meir-statman-on-coronavirus-behavioral-finance-the-second-generation-and-more/.

78 Beyond Capital, "The New Company Merging Technology, Impact, and Finance—and Offering a New Chapter for Creating Positive Change," February 12, 2020, https://www.theconsciousinvestor.co/blog/fleur-heyns-proof-of-impact.

79 Lizzie Kane, "Bryan Stephenson. 4 Steps to 'Change the World,'" City Metro, January 29, 2020, https://qcitymetro.com/2020/01/29/bryan-stevenson-4-steps-to-change-the-world/.

80 Heather C. McGhee, "Racism Has a Cost for Everyone | Heather C. McGhee," TED, May 8, 2020, https://www.ted.com/talks/heather_c_mcghee_racism_has_a_cost_for_everyone?language=en.

81 "Networks for Good: Adam Bendell of Toniic," *The Beyond Capital Podcast*, December 17, 2019, https://www.beyondcapitalpodcast.com/blog/adam-bendell.

82 "Wealth Consciousness: Seth Streeter of Mission Wealth," *The Beyond Capital Podcast*, June 16, 2020, https://www.beyondcapitalpodcast.com/blog/wealth-consciousness.

83 For more information on Jennifer Kenning, see Align's website at http://alignimpact.com/for-individuals-families-and-foundations/; or her profile on the Beyond Capital blog: http://alignimpact.com/for-individuals-families-and-foundations/.

84 The Conscious Investor, "A Guide to ESG Investing," April 23, 2020, https://www.theconsciousinvestor.co/blog/environmental-social-governance-investing.

85　Sheelah Kolhatkar, "The Ultra-Wealthy Who Argue That They Should Be Paying Higher Taxes," *The New Yorker*, December 30, 2019, https://www.newyorker.com/magazine/2020/01/06/the-ultra-wealthy-who-argue-that-they-should-be-paying-higher-taxes.

86　Certified B Corporation, "About B Corps | Certified B Corporation," Bcorporation.Net, 2019, https://bcorporation.net/about-b-corps/.

87　For more information, see: Aspiration, "Turn on Planet Protection!" 2020, https://www.aspiration.com/summit/planet-protection.

88　Banktrack, "Banking on Climate Change: Fossil Fuel Finance Report Card 2019," *2019*, https://www.banktrack.org/download/banking_on_climate_change_2019_fossil_fuel_finance_report_card/banking_on_climate_change_2019.pdf.

89　For more information, see: https://www.intersectionalenvironmentalist.com/.

90　The Impact Management Project, "Impact Management Norms," 2020, https://impactmanagementproject.com/impact-management/impact-management-norms/.

91　The International Finance Corporation, "Performance Standards," 2020, https://www.ifc.org/wps/wcm/connect/Topics_Ext_Content/IFC_External_Corporate_Site/Sustainability-At-IFC/Policies-Standards/Performance-Standards.

92　Ibid.

93　Impact Principles, "Operating Principles for Impact Management," June 2019, https://www.impactprinciples.org/sites/opim/files/2019-06/Impact%20Investing_Principles_FINAL_4-25-19_footnote%20change_web.pdfhttps://www.impactprinciples.org/.

94　World Economic Forum, "Measuring Stakeholder Capitalism: Towards Common Metrics and Consistent Reporting of Sustainable Value Creation," September 2020, http://www3.weforum.org/docs/WEF_IBC_Measuring_Stakeholder_Capitalism_Report_2020.pdf.

95　Robasciotti & Philipson, "Stop Funding Systemic Racism. This List Can Help," June 5, 2020, https://robasciotti.com/stop-funding-systemic-racism/.

96　Emma Hinchliffe, "Funding for Female Founders Increased in 2019—But Only to 2.7%," *Fortune*, March 2, 2020, https://fortune-com.cdn.ampproject.org/c/s/fortune.com/2020/03/02/female-founders-funding-2019/amp/.

97　Fesmina Faizal, "What Is Greenwashing?—Types & Examples," *Feedough*, August 4, 2019, https://www.feedough.com/what-is-greenwashing-types-examples/.

98　The Sustainability Accounting Standards Board (SASB), https://www.sasb.org/.

99　Matt Raimondi, Personal Discussion, October 7, 2020.

100 For more information, I encourage you to visit their website: https://www.divestinvest.org/.

101 David Rock and Heidi Grant, "Why Diverse Teams Are Smarter," *Harvard Business Review*, November 4, 2016, https://hbr.org/2016/11/why-diverse-teams-are-smarter.

102 For more information on the Beyond Capital Ambassador Program, please visit: https://www.theconsciousinvestor.co/blog/ambassador-program. For more information on the Acumen fund, please visit: https://acumen.org/partners/.

103 Accenture, "More Than Half of Consumers Would Pay More for Sustainable Products Designed to Be Reused or Recycled, Accenture Survey Finds," June 4, 2019, https://newsroom.accenture.com/news/more-than-half-of-consumers-would-pay-more-for-sustainable-products-designed-to-be-reused-or-recycled-accenture-survey-finds.htm.

104 John Parnell, "Half the World's Electricity Will Come from Wind, Solar, and Batteries by 2050," *Forbes*, June 20, 2019, https://www.forbes.com/sites/johnparnell/2019/06/20/half-the-worlds-electricity-will-come-from-wind-solar-and-batteries-by-2050/#465771ea7540.

105 Valerie Keller, "The Business Case for Purpose," *The Harvard Business Review*, https://hbr.org/resources/pdfs/comm/ey/19392HBRReportEY.pdf.

106 The Conscious Investor, "A Resource Guide for Beginning Impact Investors," May 8, 2020, https://www.theconsciousinvestor.co/blog/investing-the-impact-investing-resource-guide.

107 Jennifer Kenning, personal communication, December 19, 2019.

108 Sean Hinton, Soulful Convo talk series, May 2020.

109 The Conscious Investor, "My Moral Compass: Brent Kessel on Values, Mindful Consumerism, and Effectively Using Money for Good," May 1, 2020, https://www.theconsciousinvestor.co/blog/brent-kessel-abacus-wealth-values-and-money.

110 Ibid.

111 "Clothing for Conservation: Brian Linton of United by Blue," *The Beyond Capital Podcast*, May 5, 2020, https://www.beyondcapitalpodcast.com/blog/clothing-for-conservation.

112 Tatiana Schlossberg, "Moving Past Guilt—And Toward A Lower-Carbon Society | Goop," *Goop*, 2019, https://goop.com/wellness/food-planet/consumption-and-climate-change/.

113 Ibid.

114 Hans Stegeman, "There Is No Such Thing as a Neutral Investment," Triodos Investment Management, 2018, https://www.triodos-im.com/articles/2018/there-is-no-such-thing-as-a-neutral-investment.

115 For more information, see: https://www.lyft.com/careers/life-at-lyft.

116 Business Roundtable, "Redefined Purpose of a Corporation: Welcoming the Debate," *Medium*, August 25, 2019, https://medium.com/@BizRoundtable/ redefined-purpose-of-a-corporation-welcoming-the-debate-8f03176f7ad8.

117 Jon Hale, "Coronavirus Crisis Highlights Need for Stakeholder Capitalism," *Morningstar*, April 21, 2020, https://www.morningstar.com/articles/979155/ coronavirus-crisis-highlights-need-for-stakeholder-capitalism.

118 "Fashion Forward: Suzanne Lerner of Michael Stars," *The Beyond Capital Podcast*, May 19, 2020, https://www.beyondcapitalpodcast.com/blog/ fashion-forward.

119 The Conscious Investor, "Powerful Lessons on Race, Identity, and Inclusion from 4 Incredible Artists," July 2, 2020, https://www.theconsciousinvestor.co/ blog/artists-activists-race-identity-inclusion?rq=calida.

CPSIA information can be obtained
at www.ICGtesting.com
Printed in the USA
LVHW032237081121
702781LV00006B/1188